RISK AND MONEY MANAGEMENT

FOR DAY AND SWING TRADING

A complete guide on how to maximize
your profits and minimize your risks
in forex, futures and stock trading

WIELAND ARLT

TORERO TRADERS SCHOOL
GET READY FOR THE BULL

Copyright © 2020 by Wieland Arlt. All rights reserved.
Published by Torero Traders School
1st edition 2020

All rights reserved, in particular the right of reproduction and distribution as well as translation. No part of the work may be reproduced in any form or stored, processed, duplicated or distributed using electronic systems without the permission of Wieland Arlt.

Limit of Liability/ Disclaimer of Warranty: While the publisher and author have used their best efforts in preparing this book, they make no preservation or warranties with respect to the accuracy or completeness of the contents of this book and specifically disclaim any implied warranties of merchantability or fitness for a particular purpose. No warranty ma be created or extended by sales representatives or written sales materials. The advice and strategies contained herein may not be suitable for your situation. You should consult with a professional where appropriate. Neither the publisher nor author shall be liable for any loss of profit or any other commercial damages, including but not limited to special, incidental, consequential, or other damages.

ISBN: 9783982177601 (paperback)
ISBN: 9783982177618 (ebook)

For general information or your comments please send an email to:
get-ready@torero-traders-school.com
www.torero-traders-school.com

Contents

Introduction 1

PART 1:
BECOMING A PROFESSIONAL TRADER

Chapter 1: The Key to Trading Success 7

What does risk and money management have to do
with successful trading? 7

Why is risk and money management essential
for successful trading? 11

Who are you? Trader, investor, or gambler? 17

To unhinge the world:
Which trading style suits your trading account? 19

Chapter 2: Risk Management 25

Plan your trade and trade your plan!
Which elements are important for risk management? 28

All the eggs in one basket?! In this way you can
distinguish your overall risk from individual risks! 38

They always come down:
How to protect your position against losses! 44

Everything on one card? This is how you determine
your optimal position size! 49

Chapter 3: Money Management 63

From risk management to money management:
What does risk limitation have to do with determining profits? 65

Chance or risk? How to improve the quality of your trades! 69

Chapter 4: Risk and Money Management in Practice 76

Stocks, Forex and Futures—How to professionally apply
risk and money management to your trading account. 76

PART 2:
FROM BEING A PROFESSIONAL TO BECOMING A TOP TRADER

Chapter 5: Risk and Money Management Squared 87

The more, the better . . . What influence does the accuracy of your
analysis and the number of trades have on your trading success? 88

Trust your statistics . . . The significance of risk,
risk/reward ratio, hit rate, and trading frequency in practice 95

Do good things better: How to optimize your
money management and improve your trading results! 104

Chapter 6: Risk and Money Management 2.0 121

Limitation or let run? What effects does a trailing
stop have on your risk and money management? 121

Get in, get out, move up: This is how you can increase
your winnings with no change in risk!. 133

The Time-Warp: How to link different time frames 150

Chapter 7: Success Can Be Planned
In Small Steps to the Big Goal! 162

Closing words. 173

About the Author 175

About the Torero Traders School 177

Introduction

Congratulations! By reading the first lines of this book, you already belong to the circle of investors who are professionally and consciously engaged in investment and trading!

So, what does successful trading and investment involve? First, it is a robust strategy that shows you profitable opportunities. The choice of the right financial instrument is also an essential part of your success. You have the choice between stocks, ETFs (Exchange-traded funds), forex or futures—to name a few. However, the most important component of a successful investment is the conscious handling of risk and the management of your own investment capital. These are the characteristics of a professional investor and/or trader acting in the financial markets!

Although risk management is a critical consideration in investing and trading today and every investor and trader is theoretically familiar with it, in real life there is unfortunately still a huge difference whether this matter is only understood or understood and actually also applied. The results achieved by many traders often illustrate this difference in a sobering way. The professional handling of risk and the development of a positive attitude toward it make up the first part of this book.

After we have dealt intensively with the professional handling of losses we can talk about the professional handling of profits as the next step. Both—taking your losses as well as your profits—are important for a successful trader. In the past, it may have been sufficient to consider only loss limitation—i.e., risk management—in trading, but today it is equally important to consider profit taking as well. Why? On the one hand the financial markets are often enough highly volatile and suddenly jump from new highs to new lows. Sometimes, there initially shows a book profit, but a loss may eliminate it the very next moment. On the other hand, often it is not just a matter of volatility. For example, although stocks in general have always risen over time, this is not true for all stocks. Over the years, many companies and their shares have disappeared from the market without a sound—suddenly destroying the profits accumulated in the investors' accounts.

The thoughts on a conscious handling of profits lead us directly to professional money management and conclude the first part of the book.

In the second part of the book, we want to add some important elements to risk and money management and deepen the insights. In order to be successful as a trader or investor in the long term, it is important to find your own trading style and appropriate strategy and to consciously implement them. In addition, there is an almost unlimited number of trading approaches and strategies in trading and investing. What they all have in common is that their performance can be measured by certain key figures, which not only show the profit or loss achieved, but also illustrate the background of a chosen approach or implemented strategy.

Consider this example: Imagine a trader who achieves an excellent hit rate with his strategy, but takes his profits prematurely. Now imagine another trader who, with the same strategy, has the individual risk of a single position under control, but takes a too-high-overall risk due to a low hit rate. Although both traders follow the same strategy, the differences in execution and management must be taken into account accordingly when assessing performance.

This poses an essential and elementary question for active traders and investors: Where exactly are the individual levers that allow us to align our trading approaches and strategies with our capital, our experience, and the key figures we have achieved in such a way that we are able to achieve positive results on a lasting basis?

The answer to this question brings us directly to the elements of professional risk and money management. The aim of the link must be to effectively limit the risk on the one hand and to individually optimize your own trading results on the other hand, thus increasing the trading opportunities that arise.

With the "Money Management Matrix," you will get to know and use an instrument with which you can improve your personal trading results in the long term. The "Money Management Matrix" shows you the elements of professional risk and money management—with which you can adjust your trading to your individual requirements.

At this point even experienced traders will find new insights and important approaches for their personal improvement in trading.

In order to improve your money management and thus the overall trading results, we will also look at how you can reduce your risk bit by bit and thereby further protect your accumulated profits. In this context, we will also discuss a step-by-step entry and exit into and out of a position.

You can also improve your trading results by combining different time frames, as well as by gradually increasing an existing position. How exactly you can proceed here, taking into account the "Money Management Matrix" and how this affects your overall results, will also be part of this book.

In order to enable you to directly and immediately understand how the ideas and approaches presented in the book are implemented in practice, we will regularly apply them to three different account sizes and draw the appropriate practical conclusions. We will not only use different trading styles, but also different financial products in our examples.

In addition, in this book, we will also take a look behind the scenes of all trading and focus on you—the trader yourself and your mental status.

Why do that? Because ultimately, you are always behind all investment and trading decisions. For this reason, it is important that these decisions are based on your personal convictions and possibilities. Only then can you be able to implement them consistently and courageously. To find out about these personal prerequisites, the book regularly asks you to deal intensively with certain questions.

So, let us start now and determine the basic elements of your future personal trading success!

PART 1

Becoming a Professional Trader

CHAPTER 1:
The Key to Trading Success

The most important prerequisite for long-term success in investing and trading is a healthy financial basis. This is a fundamental principle. Of course, it is important not only to have this financial basis at the beginning of the trading career, but also to own and maintain it permanently. Without a financial basis, there is no trading. It's that simple. Right?

What does risk and money management have to do with successful trading?

Even though it is a foregone conclusion that the absolute prerequisite for trading is the availability of usable capital, it is important that we pay close attention to this point.

The first question that needs to be answered is to what extent professional risk and money management can help us to maintain and expand our financial base. The second question to be answered is whether there is any difference between risk management and money management and, if so, where it lies. Often both terms are used interchangeably. Everything is then regularly lumped together, according to the motto: Limiting losses has something to do with money management.

At this point, it makes sense for us to separate the two terms from each other and to consider them separately. We will then bring both terms together again in the course of the book.

In order to obtain a concrete distinction between the two terms, we generally understand risk management to be the consideration and planning of a trade or position from a risk perspective. Just to give you the conclusion: The strategy of "putting all your eggs in one basket" is not one of them. Rather, when planning a trade, you must think carefully about how much you want to spend on what. To give you a keyword already here: It is all about limiting losses and thus maintaining your financial base.

With money management, we generally combine the targeted control of the capital expenditure of your investments and the simultaneous optimal planning of the entirety of your trades with the aim of continuously increasing your financial basis. With the right money management, you can plan and control your success in the financial markets from the money side in advance. You will be surprised with the possibilities that await you!

The link between risk management and money management is the answer to the question of how much can actually be achieved with a trade or position and how this is in proportion to the potential loss. We will also discuss this point more intensively and thus be able to judge at the same time whether and to what extent a trade makes sense at all.

To get closer to risk management, let us first take a step back and become more general. At this point, let us first deal with the principle of investment in general. What does it actually mean to make an investment? Why do you invest? What do you hope to achieve by investing?

Whenever you are considering making an investment, you will probably first ask yourself what you can get back from the investment. You certainly wouldn't consider an investment if you didn't get something back, would you? At the same time, however, you will also have to deal with the risk that is inseparably linked to the investment. We know this from almost all areas of life: Where there is an opportunity, there is usually also a risk.

We can be assured that once you make an investment, you automatically take a risk. Why? Because nobody can predict the future. You invest your available resources and hope—that's all you can do—that your investment will pay off.

Did you notice? Incidentally, we are not even talking about "financial markets," "trading," or "investing." No, we are talking about an investment in general. This can go in all possible directions and does not even have to be material. Even if you help a good friend move or clean out the basement, it is an investment . . . in your friendship. And you certainly expect your friend to help you the next time you move or assemble a piece of furniture. This is, so to speak, the repayment of your investment; the certainty of being able to rely on each other is the return. But that's another matter. What is at stake here is to make it clear that, ultimately, we all invest regularly. More or less consciously, but we do.

For example, we invest time in an interesting project at work. On a private level, we invest our commitment in training for an important soccer match. Yes, we even invest in a friendship or relationship . . .

. . . and we also invest capital in promising companies or industries.

And what happens if an investment made does not pay off?

We take a risk with all investments. Namely, the risks that these investments fail and we either get nothing in return for the resources invested or, in the worst-case scenario, lose our commitment altogether: the project is cancelled, the soccer match is lost, the friendship fails, or the relationship goes to pieces. Our invested resources of time, power, and energy are lost.

Of course, we could not have known this beforehand; otherwise, we would not have gotten involved. Nevertheless, the risk of failure was always there, as was the chance of a positive outcome: the career boost after a successful project, the championship after a soccer match, the lifelong friendship or relationship.

As you can see: in the end, we invest regularly in our lives and hope that the resources we use will bring a "return" and that our investment will "pay off" for us. But we also know, of course, that we cannot always "win." Then it is simply said that nothing has happened except expenses.

Hand on heart: does that prevent us from conscientiously preparing for a new project next time, from training intensively for a soccer match again, from forming new friendly bonds again, or even from entering into a new relationship? No, of course not. But we may become a little more cautious, picky, or focused. Perhaps we will prepare ourselves even more intensively. Why? Because we want to prevent our commitment—our investment—from failing again. In a figurative sense, we practice risk management to protect ourselves against serious and excessive failures.

Now, before we go into too deep philosophical reflections on life, let's get back to the heart of the book and consider your financial investment in a promising company or industry.

And again, it is not a matter of course that your investment will work out: the company you invested in may go bankrupt or the entire industry may become outdated. In the worst case, your money—your invested capital—is lost.

Whether we like it or not, this "potential danger" is in the nature of any investment. And that's exactly why we get something back for our investment that exceeds the amount of the investment made. There's interest or dividends. Perhaps additional price gains will also tempt us to take additional risks so that our risk is worthwhile. And the higher the risk taken, the greater the potential reward for us investors must be.

This brings us directly to you. Why do you invest? Why are you trading? Why do you invest your capital? Probably in order to make a profit from it. Maybe you expect a dividend, maybe you expect interest, maybe you expect price gains. Maybe all of them together.

At this point, let's just assume that you trade stocks, currencies, or futures. What does risk and money management have to do with your successful investment—your trading?

Through risk management alone, you are already in a position to control the risks that are always associated with an investment. Risk management is the only way to transform the uncertainty associated with an investment into a certain degree of security.

And money management? What's that got to do with it? Quite simply: Where risk management saves you from being shipwrecked by an investment in trading, clever money management helps you to optimally control your trades—your investments—and to consistently build up your assets.

Both in combination are indispensable for long-term success in trading.

Why is risk and money management essential for successful trading?

You have certainly already studied the financial markets, prices, and charts in depth and are familiar with the many different patterns that can be found in a chart. Perhaps you have been following or trading the markets for a long time. Then you have certainly heard about the collapses of the world's stock markets or even experienced them personally as an investor or trader.

Before we continue here, let's go back a few years. Back in the "good old days," recommendations such as "buy a share, keep it and get rich over the years..." could be implemented with a clear conscience. The whole subject of risk management was viewed with suspicion by many, as a stock was almost risk-free in times of rising markets, flourishing economies, and bubbling profits—if you held it for a correspondingly long time. Investors and traders were able to handle this comfortably until the turn of the millennium. The only risk at that time was rather not to be present in a market or a stock.

Then the "new market" came... and everything changed!

Risk and Money Management for Day and Swing Trading

Solid companies became bankruptcy candidates, small garage companies became highly traded high flyers. Promises and ideas were worth more than concrete facts and figures. The topic of risk management was completely out of investors' focus, in the true sense of the word "out." Unfortunately, as some investors probably say in retrospect. Because the rest is history.

With the collapse of the markets, everything that was tradable went under the wheels—whether new or old economy. Nearly every share lost value dramatically. Many companies disappeared completely from the scene; some others remained in the market but have not recovered up to this day.

This is impressively demonstrated by the example of the S&P 500 Index which lost more than 50% of its value within two and a half years.

Figure 1:S&P 500 INDEX, weekly chart (one candle = one week). The S&P 500 lost 50.5% of its value from its all-time high of 1,552.87 points in 2000 to its low of 768.63 points in 2002, source: www.tradingview.com[1]

---

[1] Tradingview® is a registered trademark.

When the markets started to recover from 2002 onwards and set off for new highs, everything was, of course, quite different. The new market had disappeared and the remaining stocks and markets were all solid. International trade relations were at their peak and in the "emerging markets," double-digit growth rates per quarter had been attained for several years. The Euro was about to challenge the US Dollar as the leading currency and due to very low interest rates, many people could afford their own home even without any equity capital . . .

Almost too good to be true . . . And indeed, seven years after the crash at the turn of the millennium, the markets collapsed again with a bang. Whether stocks or commodities, everything that could be sold flew out of the portfolios. In a chain reaction, one value dragged the other down with it. In the end, what was left behind were disturbed investors, devastated portfolios, and the realization that it might be quite sensible to limit the risk of an investment.

Let us also take a look at the S&P 500 Index, which has fallen by more than its half within 1.5 years, representing the world markets.

Figure 2: S&P 500 INDEX, weekly chart (one candle = one week). The S&P 500 lost 57.69% of its value from its all-time high in 2007 at 1,576.09 points to its low in 2009 at 666.79 points, source: www.tradingview.com

Perhaps you will now say: *Well, these are the indices and, by the way, they have recovered. After all, new all-time highs in the indices have already been reached by now!* You are of course right about that, too—at least in part. Yes, the indices have recovered again; they obviously always do.

But what about the companies and their shares in the indices? Did they all recover, too?

Just let the facts speak for themselves. Using the example of the Germany Insurance Company Allianz and its share, which is regarded as a standard stock among many investors and is traded as a thoroughly sound investment, we can impressively observe that a loss of 90% has built up from the all-time high in 2000 to the low in 2003. Even though the share price moved up to €180.29 again in 2007, it still did not come close to the high of €445 in 2000. On the contrary. With the second crash in 2008 to €45.15, the share again lost a good 75% of its value.

By comparison, the German share index marked a new all-time high in 2007, thus making up for its losses within four years.

Figure 3: ALLIANZ SE, monthly chart (one candle = one month). The Allianz share lost 90% of its value from its all-time high of €445 in 2000 to its low in

2003 at 44.50. By the time it next plummeted to €45.15 in 2007, it had recovered to €180.29 before testing the low at the end of 2008 again at €45.15. Source: www.tradingview.com

There are of course other reasons to limit the risk. After all, it does not always take a global stock market crash to cause a stock to plummet. In most cases, one wrong appointment or decision in the management of a company is enough. But product cycles or fashion themes can also cause stocks to plummet just as quickly as they have rocketed them to the sky.

Think, for example, of the entire technology industry and its protagonists. Nokia shares, for example, were one of the very hot candidates in investor portfolios until technological progress overtook the company and the long decline began.

Let's take another look at the chart here:

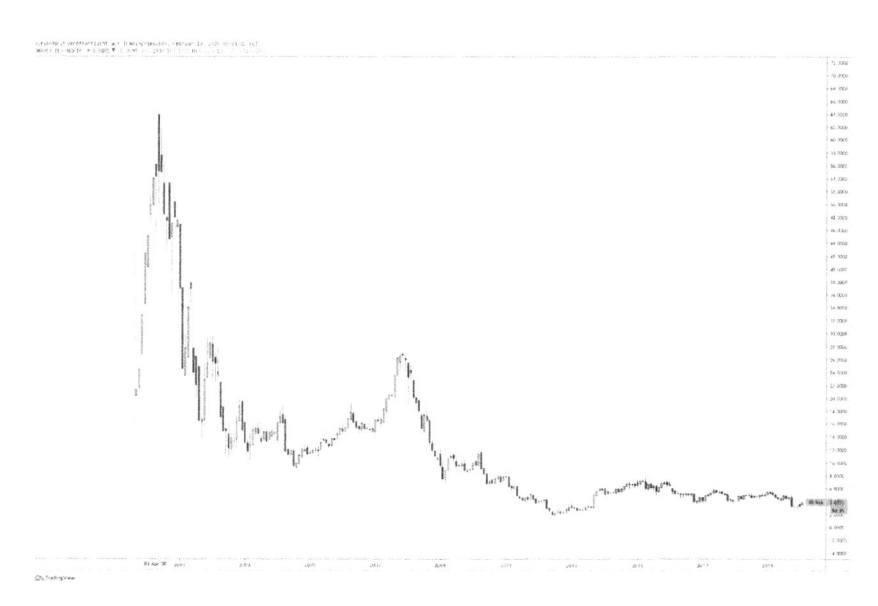

Figure 4: NOKIA CORP., monthly chart (one candle = one month). The Nokia share lost 86.45% of its value from its all-time high of €65.99 in 2000 to its low of €8.85 in 2004. After an interim recovery in 2007 to €28.66, the share fell further

to €1.33 in 2012, with Nokia losing 97.96% of its value from its all-time high in 2000. Source: www.tradingview.com

At this point we must first ask ourselves what must happen for the market to value a company at the old highs after a price loss of more than 95%? The second question that we still have to ask ourselves in this context is, in which period of time should this happen?

These two companies were of course exemplary. There are many similar examples in all indices worldwide. Without deepening the analysis of individual stocks, it should have become clear that, although stock indices regularly recover and mark new highs, their individual stocks may remain far from their highs even in recovery phases. And do so permanently.

When it comes to investment, we must always remember that the world is a fast-moving place. Trends come and go. And once they leave, they don't come back. Then there are new topics, new ideas, new products, new markets, and new winners.

Unfortunately, we always know this with absolute certainty only afterwards. True to the motto "In hindsight, you are always smarter," everything is clear and visible for everyone. In the end, unfortunately, we only know in retrospect which companies are real winners and which are permanent losers.

As a trader, you must always consider this in your investments and strictly limit the associated risk. And there is another side to the consideration—and this is where money management comes into play. Just as we don't know in advance which investment will be a loser, we can't know in advance which of the investments made will be a real winner either.

We just don't know. Despite any fundamental and/or technical analysis, we can't know. This is why it is so important that you as a trader plan your investments carefully and prepare for all eventualities. This includes not only the consideration of a possible loss but also the consideration of a possible gain. Both are important and both are essential for successful and conscious action in the markets.

Who are you? Trader, investor, or gambler?

Now that we know why it's a good idea to consider both risk and money management, we can start by looking away from the markets right to you—the person behind the trade. Only when you know from which wood you are carved can you align your risk and money management so that it suits you best and you can literally live with it.

So. Who are you—in terms of your investment behavior? Have you ever thought about how you want to trade and operate in the financial markets? Whether you prefer to take quick profits in the short term or would prefer to make a long-term commitment to the markets? Whether you are able to withstand fluctuations on the way to your big goal or you prefer to be satisfied with small profits?

If you do not have a spontaneous answer to these questions, please put the book aside for the time being and take your time to find the answers. Only when you are finished may you continue reading!

Now that you have found the first answers for yourself, you can then ask yourself the next questions that will determine your future and your success as a trader:

> Do I want to act more aggressively or defensively?
> Do I prefer to act short-term or long-term?
> How much experience do I have with my strategy in the markets I trade?
> What do I want to achieve with my actions?

This is where your risk and money management begin. You do not even need a share to do this. First of all, you only need a few quiet minutes for your inner reflection.

With your answers to these questions, you determine how you approach the market and how you operate in the market. The answers also determine what you want to do, when, and for how long. And they give you a clear goal that you want to achieve with your trading.

In the end, your answers will decide whether you will be successful in the market—or not! Your answers determine how your trading plan and strategy must be aligned and what trading style you use to trade in the markets.

For example, what does it mean when you want to act aggressively? You are then probably more willing to take a greater risk. This can mean, for example, that you enter the market a slight moment earlier or take a little more risk than a defensive trader might do. If you are more defensive, you may want to see a confirmation in the market that your entry signal is indeed valid before you take a position.

Perhaps quick success is important to you. Then you may find it difficult to hold on to a position for long and you regularly take your profits quickly. Or maybe you don't want to take quite as many positions and hold them for longer. Then you may also have to expect fluctuations during the engagement.

Perhaps you are starting trading quite fresh. Then everything is new and exciting for you. You want to try out all markets and products to find your way first. Of course, it is also possible that you are an old hand who has already seen everything that the stock exchange and the markets have to offer. You have your strategy and it has proven to be successful. You know what is coming and can control the situation at any time.

For our further procedure, it is secondary which answers you have found to the above questions for yourself, as long as you have found answers at all. So, let us assume that this is the case for our further actions.

To be able to trade successfully in the markets, you simply need to know your individual personal requirements. Your personal trading plan must be based on these.

We are thus also looking at a psychological component of trading. Always remember: You can only be successful in the markets if you pursue a strategy that is right for you and your needs. Because only then will you have full confidence in your strategy even in rough market phases and stick to them. Only if you know how and why you are trading, you will be able to consistently follow your trading. This is especially essential in hard and difficult phases of trading.

What is the connection between this "inner self-contemplation" and our topic: risk and money management? Well, on the one hand, we will go into these individual points in more detail later in the book; on the other hand, your answers also have a direct influence on how you shape your risk and money management in the future. We will also come back to this regularly in the course of the book.

Finally, you may have asked yourself why you need to set a goal that you want to achieve with your trading. The answer to this question is also simple: Only with a goal in mind can you consistently pursue this goal and align your strategy with it and maintain it.

If you don't have a goal, but operate in the markets according to the motto "being there is everything," then you will achieve exactly that. You'll be there. The danger is great that you will lose any winnings you have made without a goal in the next moment—simply because you don't know what you want to achieve and when it's time for you to stop trading. So, before you start trading, think about what you want to achieve. This prevents you from messing around aimlessly in the markets.

Therefore, once again the recommendation: Take enough time for yourself to answer the questions asked!

To unhinge the world: Which trading style suits your trading account?

We have dealt with the questions about your personal approach to trading the markets. This allows us to adapt even more individually

Risk and Money Management for Day and Swing Trading

to your personal situation and to look at the different trading styles that you can use for your trading. We want to imagine the different trading styles based on the time period in which they are traded—we can distinguish four trading styles:

POSITION TRADING: We speak of position trading when you buy a stock or title and hold it for several weeks, months, or even years. The orientation is trend-following and your goal is to stay in an existing trend as long as possible. Your analysis happens on a long-term basis using weekly and daily charts. Short-term fluctuations are less relevant for position traders than the superior trend. A dividend strategy can also be included in position trading as an additional strategy.

SWING TRADING: We want to call your activities swing trading if you trade with the trend as well as against it. Your goal in swing trading is to accompany the individual swings that a market makes from a high to a low. When the movement is complete, release your position. Accordingly, your holding period is several days or weeks. The technical analysis of the chart is mainly done in the daily chart. Regardless of this, you can, of course, follow the swings from a high to a low in a shorter or longer time frame. For our further consideration, however, swing trading should remain within the discussed period.

DAY TRADING: We speak of day-trading if you plan to hold a share or product for no more than a few hours. Overnight positions are possible if the entry to a position is found on one day and the trade is not closed until the following day. Your chart analysis as a day trader takes place in the 60-minutes chart and is supplemented by the daily chart. Whether you follow the trend in day trading or trade against it is up to you.

INTRADAY TRADING: You are an intraday trader when you execute several trades within a day and hold your positions for a few minutes up to hours. An overnight position is out of the question for you as an intraday trader. You close out all positions at the latest at the close of trading of the day and are "flat." Your technical analysis is mainly done in 60-minute, 15-minute, 5-minute, or even 1-minute charts.

You can now assign your already prepared answers to the presented trading styles. If, for example, you have stated that you are more long-term oriented, then intraday trading is less suitable for you. Position or swing trading can be a possible variant for you. Maybe you want to take your profits quickly—who knows what tomorrow will bring? Then you are probably in good hands in intraday or day trading. Or you tell yourself that you would definitely like to take your winnings with you, but that you don't want to expose yourself to the hectic pace of the day. Then you might be at home in swing trading.

It is also always a question of the amount of time you can or want to invest in your trading. If you only have a few hours a week or even weekends available, then intraday trading or day trading is rather not for you. However, there is nothing to be said against operating successfully in the markets as swing traders on a daily chart basis or as position traders on a weekly chart basis.

Finally, there are countless individual variations and combinations that you can put together from these four styles. It is important for all of them that you align your risk and money management with this and plan a trade accordingly.

At this point we can already state that swing trading or position trading requires a different risk and money management than intraday or day trading.

Since there are strong parallels between intraday trading and day trading, we will combine these two styles and work with three styles for the rest of the book: Day trading, swing trading, and position trading.

In order for you to get to know and experience these styles in a practical way, three traders would like to introduce themselves to you; they have kindly agreed to share their experiences with us. They are Rick, Anna, and Peter. Each one will trade in a different style and will trade in his or her own unique way. We will also get to know the personal backgrounds of our three traders.

It would be best if the three of them introduced themselves to you personally:

Risk and Money Management for Day and Swing Trading

Hello, my name is Rick and I work as an independent sales representative. I am twenty-seven years old, single, and have just opened my first trading account, where I have deposited $5,000. My experience in trading is limited to basic knowledge of technical analysis and observing other traders on the internet. During my working day I regularly have free time, but I have to make phone calls with my customers and business partners from time to time. I think I'll do fine as a day trader. My chart program is set on the 60-minutes chart and there I look for opportunities. As a monthly goal I have set myself a profit of $500. I would describe myself as daring and my customers know me as a salesman with a bite. Of course, I want to show my enthusiasm in trading, which is why I see myself more as an aggressive trader. For the realization of my project I see the best chances for me in the foreign exchange market. For this purpose, I have set up my account with a forex broker.

The trading target of Rick is of course very ambitious with $6,000 or 120% profit in the first year. We will see how and if he can achieve this.

Dear reader, my name is Anna. I recently received an inheritance of $25,000 and now I am faced with the challenge to "make something" out of the money. I already know my way around the stock market and shares and can look back on several years of experience in trading. Therefore, I have decided to take my financial success into my own hands. I want to use the full amount for trading. Although I already have good experience in trading, I want to act defensively in the market. You never know. My goal is to make a profit of $5,000 a year—that's a 20% growth.

Asked about her trading style, Anna replied that she wanted to become a position trader. She wants to do her technical analysis in the weekly chart and for this she reserves a few hours on the weekends. Anna wants to keep all options open and will analyze both the world's indices and individual stocks from them and trade them directly on the respective stock exchanges. Anna is thirty-five years old and married.

Good afternoon, my name is Peter. I work as a department manager in a large company and I am forty-eight years young. As a manager I am quite busy during the day, but nevertheless I have been able to read a lot about trading in the last few months and have discussed with my family about opening a trading account of $15,000 with a futures broker. A first test with *a demo account already went well and I am confident that I can achieve a profit of 10% to 15% per year with swing trading. As a responsible father of two children, I want to approach trading defensively. I have arranged with my family that I will be given one hour every evening to take care of my positions. My technical analysis takes place in the daily chart. For my trading I use futures.*

Expressed in concrete figures, Peter's trading target is $1,500 to $2,250 profit in the first year. Here, too, we will see how Peter applies his risk and money management to achieve his goals.

Anna, Rick and Peter will accompany us from now on and are kind enough to share their ideas, experiences, and thoughts with us regularly.

This will enable us to conclude our preparatory deliberations and take the next step towards professional risk management.

A brief summary of the most important facts:

> Risk management and money management are two terms that should be considered separately.
> Risk management serves to limit losses.
> Money management comprises the control and improvement of trading results through targeted planning of capital deployment and other elements.
> Investments are always associated with a risk of failure. Risk management supports you in limiting this risk.
> Although stock indices regularly recover over time after slumps, this does not apply to all companies included. After a collapse over a long period of time, equities often lag behind their highs. Risk management avoids holding on to weak companies and paves the way for investments in new potential winners.
> Shares can crash together with an index, but also on their own initiative. Especially the technical analysis can help you to avoid high losses and find a timely exit from loss positions.

Risk and Money Management for Day and Swing Trading

> Before you open a trading account and enter the markets, it is necessary to know about yourself. Only if you know where your personal strengths and preferences in trading lie can you start your trading upon them. This is also part of professional risk management.

> The choice of the appropriate trading style is also part of this. Whether you want to act in the long or short term is your individual decision and has an impact on the design of your risk and money management.

CHAPTER 2:
Risk Management

The examples from the previous chapter should be enough to make it clear that you cannot avoid professional risk limitation in trading. In fast-moving markets, where investment decisions require regular review, you need to make sure that you do not suddenly have a long-term and permanent loss-maker in your portfolio.

But how can you ensure this? How can you identify such a "performance killer"?

Certainly, there are methods in fundamental and especially in technical analysis that can indicate a long-term loser. If, for example, a company's new product launch fails or the business figures turn out worse than expected for several quarters in a row, then from a fundamental point of view it is at least advisable to take a closer look at the chart and check to what extent an investment still makes sense at all. Unfortunately, in such a case, the share has normally already gone a long way down. So, anyone waiting for the fundamental data of a company—to speak clearly—will often be in for a nasty surprise and, in case of doubt, will have to take heavy losses before she or he pulls the emergency brake and removes the share from her or his portfolio.

Perhaps technical analysis gives better and faster indications when a share or a market in general is heading south. And indeed, there are many clues that make a hint here and there. For example, the break through an important support or the finalization of a top formation can be a first signal to leave the sinking ship. A shoulder-head-shoulder formation, for example, gives clear indications that something is wrong with a market or share. When the market shows the first signs of weakness and does not reach another new high after a high, the first investors become nervous. If a share then also falls below an important support level, then the probability is high that it will continue to fall, at least in the short term.

Let's take a look at a chart with a typical shoulder-head-shoulder formation:

Figure 5: S&P 500 INDEX, weekly chart (one candle = one week). The S&P 500 rises from its low in 2009 at 666.79 points to its high in 2011 at 1,370.58 points. There it forms a head which is only slightly higher than the previous high - the left shoulder. When the S&P 500 does not create a new high, the right shoulder forms. With breaking the neck line at point 1, the sale starts at 1,265 points. The S&P 500 loses around 15% of its value within three months. Then the S&P 500 stabilizes and begins a new rally to a new all-time high. Source: www.tradingview.com

We see that the S&P 500 has been on an uptrend since 2009. After a steady and direct rise, the S&P 500 falls back, rises again and forms a new high. So far so good. This also fits into the overall picture. But then something happens that does not fit into the big picture. The S&P 500 falls, begins to rise again and then suddenly doesn´t form a new high. At this moment chart technique becomes really interesting! At this point we can interpret a little bit. What is happening in the minds of investors? After a rise over several months or years, suddenly no new high? In the area of the all-time high?! What's going on there?!

We do not need to be clairvoyants to know that a reaction at this point is at least likely. Caution is now more than appropriate! And indeed: In accordance with the market rule "what cannot rise, must fall," the S&P 500 is heading south. It first breaks through the support at point 1 and then the support at point 2.

Let us pause for a moment at this point and consider the facts:

1. The market does not manage to mark a new high, but bounces back in the area of the all-time high.
2. After a long rally the price comes to a halt and the first important support is broken through.

What would your reaction be? What do you expect? After the experiences of 2000 and 2007, what is your first impulse?

That's how many people think! After breaking through point 2, the price went clearly down again. Investors have exited their positions and short sellers have also entered the market. Both of these factors caused the S&P 500 to drop below 1,100 points within a few months.

So, can chart technique provide indications of trend reversals? Yes, it can! But they are only clues. We can also see that the S&P 500 rose again immediately after the sell-off, reaching a new all-time high in the process.

So isn´t it better to hold on to the position? Sitting out the losses? Obviously, things are always going up after all! Here we have to think about our risk management. After the experiences of the past: Who could say in advance where the sellout would end? We cannot predict the future and therefore must protect ourselves against elementary losses.

Therefore, in such situations there can only be one recommendation to you: Get out of the market!

Risk management primarily means limiting losses. And those who, for example, have closed out their positions at point 1 or even point 2 have saved themselves a large part of the losses. And a saved loss is in this sense also a gain!

Why exactly is it better to drop out than to stay in this position and hope for better times? Because we simply do not know how far a sellout will go and when the recovery will finally take place.

In this way, you keep your valuable trading capital together, which ultimately forms the basis of your trading.

Let's think one step further: you have a strict risk management policy and may have exited the market at point 1 or 2. In the course of your regular market analysis, you will then discover that the sellout has not gone as far as you feared. Who is to prevent you from getting back in after the first signs of recovery? A first opportunity to do so is given, for example, in point 3.

Once again: Risk management means limiting losses!

Plan your trade and trade your plan! Which elements are important for risk management?

Now that you are so intensively attuned to loss limitation and risk management, it is important to concretize things after the general considerations. The first step towards professional risk management is the appropriate planning of a trade under risk aspects. In order to get an idea of what risk in trading actually means and how much risk is allowed, please take a look at the following table:

Loss	Recovery	Recovery to loss ratio
10%	11.10%	1.11
20%	25.00%	1.25
30%	42.90%	1.43
40%	66.70%	1.67
50%	100.00%	2
60%	150.00%	2.5
70%	233.30%	3.33
80%	400.00%	5
90%	900.00%	10
95%	1900.00%	20

Figure 6: The long way back. Where a first small loss can be made up without much effort, the tide begins to turn with increasing losses. Once the 50% are exceeded, you must make at least 100% profit to get back to the starting point. If you have lost 95% of your trading account, you need 1,900% profit to get back to zero.

What does this table tell us? We now know that trading is not just about making profits. Losses are always part of trading. This is unavoidable and simply part of the business—the running costs, so to speak. As we know from good merchants, it is also important for us to keep the costs as low as possible. You can see from the table what it means when costs get out of hand, i.e., when losses take over.

Let's assume you have a trading account with a $10,000 deposit and you invest this $10,000 in a single title. Despite careful planning, you have to accept a 10% loss on this one stock. What does this mean for your trading account? You have lost exactly $1,000 after the loss of 10%, which you are now missing on your trading account. This means that you will only have $9,000 available for your next purchase. So, you buy the next share for a total of $9,000. This time you are on the right side and achieve a profit of 11% with your trade. With this 11% gain, you can make up for your loss and return to the starting point of your account.[2] With a loss of 10% in the back, to achieve a profit of 11% in the next step and thus return to the initial value is manageable and within the bounds of possibility. Even with a loss of 20%, we can assume that a halfway skillful trader will not be put off by this and will be able to make up for this loss within a reasonable time. But from a 30% loss on, things slowly start to look different. The further you get into the loss zone, the greater the challenge to get out of it and at least balance the trading account again. Even a loss of 50%—whether with one trade or in total—means that you have to double your trading account to get back to the starting point.

Assuming you succeed in doing so, the question immediately arises: why you did not double your account from the very beginning?

The further you get into the loss zone, the harder the way back becomes and you get deeper and deeper into the inability to act. Once you have lost 80% of your trading account, you need to earn 400% more to make up for it. Related to your account with the original $10,000 this means that with $2,000 left you have to make a profit of $8,000. A mature performance that will definitely include you in the circle of top traders.

If this seems impossible, then it becomes even utopian in the range from a 90% loss. Whoever still achieves 900% or even 1,900% profit with his back against the wall belongs in the Olympus of the traders.

But joking aside, the whole thing has a very serious background. The conclusion from this is that you must avoid slipping below 30% into the loss zone under all circumstances. In fact, you prefer to stay above the 20% loss limit. To stay with our example, the challenge for you is then "only" to achieve a profit of $2,000 with $8,000.

---

[2] Please note that it is not exactly $1,000 profit, but $990. Strictly speaking, the percentage for recovery is 11,1 $\overline{\%}$. Let's round it off here for simplicity's sake. This does not change the basic findings and we keep things simple. Incidentally, we have also left out all transaction costs for our consideration.

For this reason, the key factor in risk management is the risk taken in each case. Let us put this into practice right away: Answer the following question and please be honest with yourself:

> How much risk am I willing to take per trade or position?

Of course, there are formulas and rules of thumb for this, which we will also look at below. But now the main thing is that you determine an amount that is right for you. This is a purely individual answer and has only to do with your personal well-being and there is a reason for this.

This is because in the event of a loss, the amount you have specified is away from your account and will be recorded as a loss. This means that you cannot buy a new share for this amount. This means that you cannot go on holiday from this amount. This also means that if you are in doubt, this amount is not available for your personal needs.

If you are already experiencing abdominal pain, then that is a good thing. Because it is good to think intensively during the preparation and then act consciously. So, if you are in any way concerned about your capital: Nobody forces you to take full advantage of the risk in trading.

Only if you choose an amount that suits you and that you can cope with in case of a loss, you can be sure that you will take the trade boldly at the moment of opening the position. And only with the right amount of risk for you, you are mentally able to analyze the situation calmly and prudently in the event of a loss and to make further professional decisions.

So just to be on the safe side, how much risk are you willing to take per trade?

Of course, there is also a concrete variant for determining the risk to be taken, which ideally also corresponds to your considerations in the result. To do this we need to look at your overall financial situation. In order to determine an optimal amount of risk, we need a concrete overview of your assets. In practice, the definition of assets is quite broad. There are voices that count real estate, insurance, jewelry, and other valuables as assets. This is certainly correct for the term "assets," but it does not help us in our considerations here.

For our purposes, we therefore want to deal with all your liquid assets:

> How much liquid funds are available for your trading?
> How much of this will you use for trading and deposit to your trading account?

This two-pronged approach of trading account on the one hand and other liquid assets in reserve on the other hand makes sense, for example, if you do not want to fill your trading account with 100% of your cash assets, but are basically willing to use them.

At this point, let us make sure that you only use the cash you can spare for trading.

Under no circumstances should you put all your eggs in one basket, but always keep a liquidity reserve with which you can start trading again in an emergency. Always keep an eye on your personal retirement provision. This is also part of professional risk and money management!

So, let us assume that you have a precise record of your liquid cash assets and you have the part reserved for trading on your trading account. Let us further assume that you have deposited the aforementioned $10,000 into your trading account. These $10,000 are from now on the basis for our further considerations.

In practice, an amount dependent on the trading account has proven to be a good way of determining the risk to be taken. Many traders take an amount of 1% to 2% of their trading account here. Of course, you can also take an amount that is less than 1%, for example 0.5% of your trading account. This always depends on the size of your trading account. When determining your risk amount, always take into account the fact that a loss also needs to be compensated. And as we have already stated above, the deeper you are into the overall loss, the longer and more difficult the way back is.

Therefore, keep the 2% as the maximum upper limit of your risk!

Surely at this moment you have already guessed what this realization means for you. We had already discussed which risk amount is the right one for you without knowing the percentage rule of thumb. Now, if you compare one amount with the other:

> Which amount is higher?
> Which amount is the more convenient for you?
> Which amount are you more comfortable with? Mentally and financially?
> What amount of money will let you sleep well even if you stay in your position overnight?

Make your decision. For your own calculations, you will find below the formula for the amount at risk per position:

$$Trading\ account * Risk\ in\ percent = Risk\ amount$$

In relation to our sample account, this means

$$\$10,000 * 1\% = \$100$$

Regardless of the percentage, you should rather choose the amount that makes you feel good and lets you sleep well at night. In order to calculate the percentage amount from this absolute amount, we have to change the formula a little bit:

$$\frac{Risk\ amount}{Trading\ account} = Risk\ in\ percent$$

If you have decided on an amount of—for example—$75 as the risk to be taken, then this means in relation to your trading account:

$$\frac{\$75}{\$10,000} = 0.0075 = 0.75\%$$

Determining the percentage risk on your trading account is important because this value determines the initial amount you start trading with. You can easily imagine that the development of your trading account is anything but static. On the contrary, development will be dynamic—in both directions. By choosing a percentage risk amount you ensure that you always enter the market with the same risk in relation to your trading account. So, if you can increase your trading account from $10,000 by 10% to $11,000, then your risk to be taken will also increase by 10%.

The calculation then looks like this:

$$\$11,000 * 1\% = \$110$$

The percentage risk remains unchanged. Not the absolute risk. The absolute risk develops together with your trading account. Assuming you suffer a 10% loss on your trading account, the risk calculation for your next trade will look like this:

$$\$9,000 * 1\% = \$90$$

In this way you ensure that you always trade within the appropriate limits and that your risk does not become disproportionately high compared to the trading account. Because if you kept the absolute amount constant, you would very quickly become incapacitated if you lost.

Even if you are guided by your "feel-good" amount, the recommendation is to convert it to the percentage amount from your trading account. As the account grows, this amount will, of course, also increase in absolute terms. In case of a win, the original $75 will quickly become $80 or $90 and you are, of course, free to reduce the percentage amount and stay with your desired amount. The flip side of the coin, however, is that it literally slows down an essential element of money management and thus slows down the growth of your trading account. Of course, you must be aware of this in this procedure.

In summary, we can say that determining the percentage risk as a function of the size of the trading account in good times with profits steadily increases the absolute amount at risk, which in turn increases the trading account. In bad times with several losses in a row, the percentage determination of the risk slows down the decline by steadily decreasing absolute risk amounts. In this way, you ensure that you always remain capable of acting and protecting your valuable capital, even in phases with multiple losses—so-called "draw-down phases."

At this point, we could conclude our considerations regarding the risk to be taken and move on to the next point. However, let us stay with this topic a little longer and at the same time continue to focus on you and your strengths.

In the first chapter, we dealt with the question of whether you want to trade aggressively or defensively and also questioned how much experience you already have in the markets and products you trade. The question was also asked whether you are more long-term or short-term oriented. There were very specific reasons for this. At this point we can come back to these points. Please take a look at your answers again.

Why does it make sense to have concrete answers for oneself in terms of determining the amount of risk?

When determining the amount at risk, you must also take into account your personal circumstances. Sure, the trading account forms the basis of your calculations. However, this is only a first recommendation, one which you should not implement rigidly and without questioning and without comment. If, for example, you have determined that you would rather trade defensively in the market, then it is worth considering reducing the percentage risk amount a little—for example, from 1% to 0.75% or even to 0.5%.

If you just stick strictly to the above formula, there is a risk that you will not feel comfortable about in your "trader skin" and that trading will be rather uncomfortable for you from the very beginning. For this reason, it is important to include this aspect in the determination of risk.

You must also include your experience in the markets or products you trade in the risk assessment. Imagine that you are completely new in the financial markets. Perhaps you do not yet know the trading platform, the markets, or the products one hundred percent and you are just starting to trade. As in real life, the motto is "learning by doing." What does this mean for your risk management? Of course—keep the risk small! Again, the percentage calculation is used as a first orientation. But if you are new to a topic, there can only be one recommendation for you: Reduce your risk! Take a 0.5% risk or even less. As your experience grows, you can then increase the percentage risk bit by bit.

At the beginning of your career, it is important to buy the experience you need as cheap as possible. Always remember that no one is forcing you to trade at full risk. Make your experiences until you are absolutely confident in your chosen markets, strategies, and products. Then further adjust your risk to the new level of experience.

Let us now leave the theoretical part and look at the practical side. There Peter, Anna, and Rick are already waiting to share their thoughts with us. Let Rick be the first to speak:

I only have a small trading account. If I calculate my risk correctly, then with one percent risk of the trading account, the absolute risk is only $50. I'm not really getting anywhere with this, but . . . I am sure I will soon be able to take more absolute risks!

Rick is understandably disappointed with his absolute amount at risk. Many traders start their trading with ideas of the very large amounts—as profit. It is the strict and constant limitation of risk that makes a trader permanently successful. And as Rick also says: Soon the absolute amount will be larger and then the "big profits" will come. With regard to the trading market and the trading style, it should be said that—especially in forex trading—it is possible to trade in the short term with a relatively low amount of risk.

How does Anna approach the determination of her risk?

With my trading account of $25,000, I can really make a difference. My risk is $250 per trade and position with one percent of $25,000. I can deal with this, especially since I plan for a longer period of time in position trading anyway and am not as strongly affected by random fluctuations as a trader acting at short notice. I feel comfortable with this and I am also thinking about increasing my risk to 1.5% depending on the situation.

As a position trader, Anna will not execute as many trades as a day trader. The overall risk assessment for Anna will also be based on a longer period of time. When Anna says that she wants to increase her risk to 1.5% depending on the situation, it seems appropriate for her trading style and account.

Finally, let us listen to Peter's thoughts:

I am torn. Actually, I trust myself with everything. A 1% risk from my account is $150. To have or not to have. I don't want to risk too much and I'd better take it slow. I will initially set myself at 0.75% risk. So, my absolute risk at the beginning is at $112.50 maximum. I think I can handle it better.

Peter is reserved, although he already had good experiences with the demo account. Since Peter considers himself defensive, this strategy will also suit him well.

Let us look at the statements again in a tabular overview:

	Rick	**Anna**	**Peter**
Trading Style	Day Trading	Position Trading	Swing Trading
Account size	$5,000	$25,000	$15,000
Product	Forex	Shares, ETF	Futures
Percentage risk per trade	1.00%	1% - 1,5%	0.75%
Absolute risk per trade	$50	$250 - $375	up to $112

Figure 7: Overview of the three traders Rick, Anna and Peter and their initial situations

Risk and Money Management for Day and Swing Trading

Let us take up the previous idea directly and go into the subject of risk management in greater depth:

All the eggs in one basket?! In this way you can distinguish your overall risk from individual risks!

This section may surprise you. On closer inspection, however, it is the logical next step in our consideration. So far, we have discussed the risk to be taken, but this only applies per trade and position.

What is also important for your success planning and risk management is the question of overall risk. Once again, you now have the opportunity to deal specifically with another question:

> How much overall risk is acceptable for me?

Before you answer lightly here, please think back and consider how much profit you need to make up for your losses.

It is easy to say that you can cope with a loss of 2%, 3% or 5%. Or that you say: *I still can accept a $1,000 loss. That's factored into my risk planning.*

But what does it look like when we no longer talk about a single losing trade, but a series of losing trades? Can you still be so bold saying that this was also calculated?

You must always be aware that every strategy simply involves not only individual losses, but entire series of losses. Then it is perfectly normal that four, five, six or even more losing trades occur in a row. And then the losses add up to an overall loss. Professional risk management is also and especially in demand here. Anyone can handle a losing trade ... but dealing professionally with a series of losses is a completely different matter. To do this, it is important that you have a plan of what you are going to:

1. accept as a total risk
2. and do when this amount of total risk is reached.

The answer to the first question is again a very individual answer. Here, too, it is all about "feeling good." You must be able to deal with the accumulated losses at all times. A good indicator of the acceptable level of total losses is, incidentally, your family or spouse. Can you imagine to openly address your losses: *Dear darling, I currently have a $15,000 loss on my trading account* . . .

If not, then in any case you already know which amount is too high. What reads jokingly at first is unfortunately often the bitter truth. In order to intensify the unpleasant effects, an additional psychological point is added to the financial loss. If the overall losses become too high, you will not only be financially incapacitated, but also mentally. There is then a danger that you will go into shock, so to speak, and miss the trading opportunities that could lead you out of the losing path. You then not only lack the financial basis for action, but also the belief in the market, your strategy, and ultimately in yourself.

From this moment on, there is a great danger that you either hang up trading—which would be a pity—or that you get the idea of "taking revenge" on the market and with the courage of desperation throw good money after bad money—which would also be a pity.

For this reason, it is important to conduct risk management professionally and to think seriously about what overall loss is acceptable as well as financially and mentally bearable for you.

Unfortunately, there is no rule of thumb that could be presented here. In practice, there are traders for whom the fifth loss in a row is the end, others draw their limit at the already mentioned 10% total loss from their trading account. As already said, it is a purely individual decision.

The next question that follows is what you do when your loss limit is reached. Many traders then stop trading immediately and start analyzing the market and their own trading. If you experience a series of losses, then the same is recommended to you.

The reason is simple. If your proven trading strategy suddenly fails several times in a row, then something is different than usual. This can be due to the market, but also to you. Under the given circumstances, trading then no longer makes any sense. Instead, you should search for the causes. Analyze your trading market, your methodology, and/or your personal condition and pause until your inner condition, the market, and your methodology fit together again.

Risk management, therefore, means not only limiting the risk of a single position, but also thinking in advance about how you want to deal with a series of losses and at what point you want to temporarily interrupt your trading.

To complete the picture, we need to look at two other aspects of overall risk.

Imagine you are a position trader like Anna. The market is doing well and you are fully invested in the market with your trading account. You have ten stocks in your portfolio of which you are 100% convinced. What do you need to be aware of?

When planning your overall positions, you must of course also keep the overall risk of your portfolio in mind! Especially if you want to act as a swing or position trader in the long term. When planning your overall risk, always consider the way back. Especially when it comes to the overall risk, you must not risk your ability to act. This is particularly important given the impressions of the past few years, when we have already experienced two global market collapses in quick succession. Set an amount that is acceptable to you and when that amount is reached, exit the market and liquidate your positions. Then watch the nervous activity of the remaining market participants, relaxed from the sidelines and look for profitable entry opportunities when the storm has passed. When others then still check their shrunken bank accounts in disbelief, you have again entered the market with almost full force. That is professional risk management!

With these considerations up to date, the vast majority of traders conclude their risk assessment and plunge into trading. One short-term as an intraday trader, the other long-term as a position trader. In this context, however, we still have to consider a final aspect of risk management.

We have already stated above that in practice, a risk per trade and position of 1%–2% of the trading account has proven to be a good practice. But does this also apply to all trading styles?

Suppose you want to be an intraday trader. Then what about your percentage position size? Does the rule of thumb of 1%–2% of the trading account also apply here? Probably not. You must always keep the time reference in mind. An intraday trader has a different trading frequency than a position trader. The position trader converts a fraction of the trades of an intraday trader. Of course, the two cannot take the same risks—neither in percentage nor absolute terms.

Imagine that in numbers. Let's assume you have a trading account with a $100,000 deposit and want to act as an intraday trader. Do you want to take $1,000 as absolute risk per trade? After a series of losses of five trades in a row, you have - roughly rounded: a total loss of $5,000 or 5%. If you are trading on the 1-minute chart, you won't need ten minutes to trade in the worst-case scenario. Regardless of what your nerves may be like afterwards, this approach is a good way to eliminate a trading account in a short period of time.

So, the more short-term you act in the market, the lower the percentage risk that you have to take per position. The large number of possible trades in short-term trading alone means that you otherwise run the risk of keeping the overall risk disproportionately high. Conversely, you can increase the percentage risk slightly the longer you want to be active in the market. This is simply due to the fact that with longer-term investments you can execute fewer trades in the course of the year than a short-term oriented trader.

And of course—as we already mentioned in the first chapter—professional risk management also includes not investing the entire trading account in a single stock or market, but rather—and this is where the percentage risk per position in combination with the overall risk comes into play—that a sensible diversification takes place in your portfolio. This means that you mix industries, countries, regions, and, ideally, also currencies in your portfolio.

This means that we can now actually conclude our reflections on risk management and once again look to the practical side. What do our three traders say? Let's start with Rick right away:

As a day trader in the forex market, I am less embarrassed to think about a portfolio structure. But what seems important to me is to be careful not to accidentally trade the same direction with different pairs at the same time. I am careful to trade currency pairs that are not equal and in line to each other. Otherwise, I have decided to take a break for the rest of the week after losing five trades in a row. If this happens, I go into intensive analysis. As a maximum overall risk, I consider 15% of the trading account as realistic. If that is reached, I will definitely end the month. Instead, I then switch to a demo account to improve my skills without any further risk. But since I want to win, this is just a theoretical consideration for me . . .

Rick is right in his assessment. In the forex market, too, there are currency pairs going in line with others, which should actually be treated as a single trade and overstretch the risk management. The 15% overall risk corresponds to his aggressive assessment. It is important that Rick takes a break when he reaches his 15%, conducts an intensive market analysis, and questions himself and his actions. An interesting idea is to continue trading, but to use a demo account. Thus, Rick remains active in the market, but no longer takes any further risks.

What is the design of the overall risk for Anna?

I stick with the classic 10% overall risk. I like the remark about diversification and I will take it into account in my analysis. In this way, I avoid the risk of investing too much in one industry or area. I will do the retrospective analysis after each trade anyway and I regularly observe the markets on the weekend. For me, 10% total risk is more of a limit than the number of losses in a row. Once I reach 10%, I'll definitely take a break for the trading month.

As Anna moves on the weekly chart as a position trader, she has a long-term focus. Whether she stops trading after reaching the 10% loss limit or after a certain number of consecutive losses is, of course, her decision.

Finally, let us look over Peter's shoulder:

That's a hot one. I think if I had to confess to my family that I just lost $1,500, it would be hard for me. I'm more likely to pull the ripcord for me. For me, the trading month is definitely over after a 5% overall loss. I also have to cope with a $750 loss first of all by myself. I don't want that to happen. Actually, I already have a bad feeling after four losses in a row. Then I have to sit down and analyze my strategy and the markets. I do the same with the demo account, so I can immediately see when my trading ideas and the markets are matching again while staying in training.

Peter is defensive and pays attention to his personal financial and mental comfort zone. This ensures that he remains emotionally stable, confident in making decisions and capable of acting.

We can complete our tabular overview:

	Rick	Anna	Peter
Overall risk in percentage	15.00%	10.00%	5.00%
Overall risk in US Dollar	$750	$2,500	$750

Figure 8: The overall risks of our traders Peter, Anna and Rick at a glance

We have now discussed loss limitation and risk minimization in detail. It becomes clear that in trading, you have to protect against the individual risk of a position in any case, but that you should also be careful about the overall risk.

So far, these have been rather abstract ideas and concepts. Let us now go further and look at methods and possibilities that support you in professionally designing your risk management.

They always come down: How to protect your position against losses!

Risk management means limiting losses. Hopefully, you have now internalized this principle and it will help you in trading to protect and maintain your financial base. However, this principle alone will only help you to a limited extent. Because what you now know is that you only limit your risk to the extent that you will have to step out of your position at some point. But that doesn't really sound like a plan yet. In the next step, we want to determine when the point is reached where it makes no sense to hold on to your position any longer and you have to end your trade.

For this purpose, it is important to note that trading is based on probabilities. Since we cannot predict the future—we already have come so far in our considerations—we must inevitably orient ourselves by probabilities. When analyzing a stock or a market, everything ultimately comes down to one question: In which direction will the stock or market move next with the greatest probability? That's the bottom line. There are a number of methods of analysis for this, which are located somewhere between art, science, and esotericism. What they all have in common is the goal of being able to make a statement about the probability of a market moving next in one direction or the other. This is obviously quite vague, of course, and that is precisely why you practice strict risk management—namely, to limit the losses if the market takes the wrong direction for you, contrary to the assumed greater probability.

Now, when planning a trade, the next question already arises: At what point is it no longer likely that your stock or market will take the direction you prefer?

When considering whether to make a trade, you must therefore make a decision based on probabilities rather than facts. If you then decide to go into the market, you make a decision under uncertainty at the same time. The uncertainty here lies in not knowing whether the trade will be a winner or a loser. You just can't know. You must be content with the probabilities. But whether these are then also true, you simply still do not know.

It is your task as a professional trader to turn the uncertainty that exists in trading into certainty in your planning. This certainty lies in knowing that you either win or lose. You can assume this without the slightest doubt in advance.[3] We can further specify this certainty. What can you already say with absolute certainty through your preparations?

You already know when you open a trade what you can lose at most under normal circumstances. You have already determined this amount. This amount is sure for you.

Now all you have to do is incorporate these considerations into your planning by bringing things together:

1. You plan a trade based on probabilities. Therefore, there must be a point where the probability that your idea will work out is no longer given—that is, zero.
2. At this point, you know the maximum you have lost, which is your fixed risk per trade.

This point is your initial stop loss, which you set when planning a position and put into the market after opening the trade. This is the point at which you realize your losses and the trade is closed without hesitation.

There are several ways to determine the stop loss. Long-term investors in particular often say that they don't want to pin this down so precisely on a price, but rather on the fundamentals. This is dangerous in that the market may already have fallen strongly at the point where the fundamentals have changed significantly. We already talked about this.

Then there are traders who set percentage stops. For example, they say, *After a 5% loss, I'll pull out of the stock!* This is, of course, very general and can be in the middle of a correction, which does not necessarily endanger the original idea and does not question the probability of success. It would be a pity if you have to get out of a position in the

---

[3] We leave out of consideration an analysis in which the exit takes place at the entry price. This would require an active management of the position and thus an intervention in the trade.

middle of a correction. The same applies if you take an absolute stop loss in the form of a fixed amount of money instead of a percentage stop loss. Such a blanket approach has not proven itself in practice and also regularly leads to suboptimal results.

In practice, on the other hand, stops according to chart criteria have proven to be effective. This procedure has the advantage that not only the entry but also the exit can be determined according to chart criteria. Please take this opportunity to pick up any chart you like. What do you see?

You will find that a price moves in regular swings. It goes in one direction, then again in the other, only to run in the original direction again in the next swing. If in this way new highs are regularly created, followed by rising lows, we speak of an uptrend. On the other hand, we speak of a downtrend when new lows are constantly being reached with the swings, followed by ever lower highs. Figures 9 and 10 show these swing movements in the model:

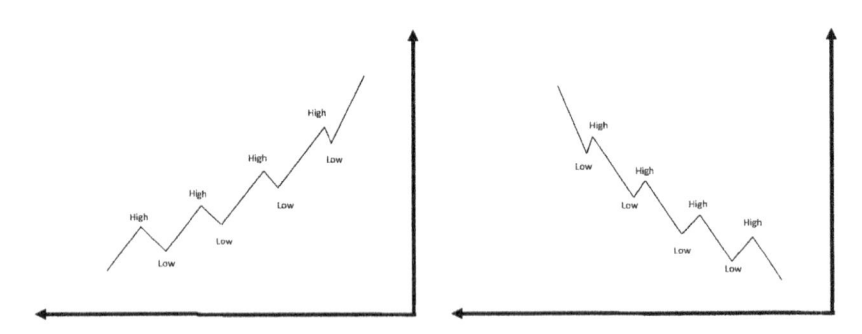

Figure 9 and 10: An uptrend with higher highs and higher lows and a downtrend with lower highs and lower lows.

Up to this point, we had always assumed that you, as a buyer, were trading in an uptrend. Of course, you can also trade the other direction—i.e., as a seller in a downtrend. For what has been said, this ultimately means the same thing with different signs. In order not to complicate things unnecessarily, we want to maintain this original assumption in the future.

Chart analysis is particularly useful for determining which direction a price is most likely to go in its next movement. You can then use a chart to determine the point at which it becomes unlikely that the price will move in a certain direction.

For an uptrend, for example, we can say that the probability of the trend continuing is close to zero the very moment the price has broken through the last low point downwards. The sequence of rising high points and rising low points has thus effectively been ended. Here you can place your stop loss.

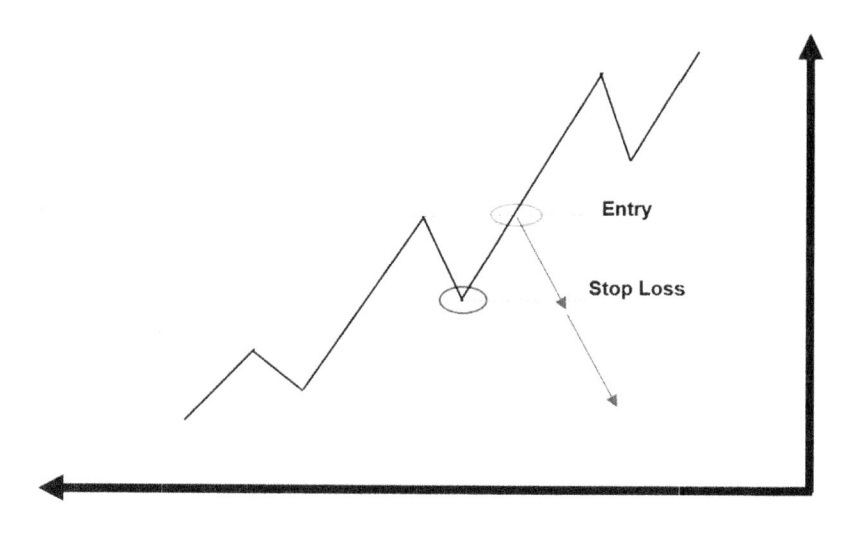

Figure 11: Entry and stop loss in the model. The stop loss is set where the probability that the trading idea will still work out is no longer given. When the last low is broken, the sequence of rising highs and rising lows comes to an end and the trend is at least threatened.

What can the placement of a stop loss look like in practice? For this we take a look at the Dow Jones Industrial Index:

Risk and Money Management for Day and Swing Trading

Figure 12: DOW JONES INDUSTRIAL INDEX, daily chart (one candle = one day). The Dow Jones has fallen back to point 1 and then recovers to the resistance zone at point 2, where the index corrects to point 3 and then rises further. A new uptrend has been established following the breakout. Source: www.tradingview.com

Most traders want to enter a new trend at the earliest possible time. After marking a low at point 1, the Dow Jones Industrial Index rose to the resistance level at point 2. As expected, the index fell again from there. To continue the downtrend, the index would have had to break through point 1. But it didn't. Instead, the correction stopped at point 3, forming a higher low than at point 1. Obviously, market participants do not want to sell their positions at this point and there seems to be additional buying power from other market participants. At point 3, the Dow Jones begins to rise again. To get into the beginning trend early, point 2 is a good orientation. A good entry point would be the crossing of the last high at point 2 and a simultaneous break of the resistance.

With this, we would have already determined the starting point.

Next, we need to determine at what point in the chart it no longer makes sense to speculate on further rising prices. This is point 3 on the

Dow Jones chart, and if the index falls below this point, the index will set out to mark a new low below the previous one. This point forms our stop loss. If this point is undershot, we will exit our position in order to avoid major losses.

Now you know when to enter the position and you also know when your stop loss should take effect and you can exit the market again. Since in practice, there is unfortunately regularly a difference between knowing and doing, the urgent recommendation to you is to place the stop loss in the market immediately after opening the position. This is no challenge with today's trading platforms and can actually be done with the entry order already. This has two advantages for you: You are relieved mentally as well as temporally, so you don't have to sit in front of the PC all day long and you don't run the risk of hesitating or wanting to reinterpret the chart at the moment of action.

In dealing with stop losses, it is important to note that under no circumstances may they be taken out of the market or shifted to your disadvantage. A stop loss serves as your personal loss limitation and protects you against unplanned losses. Even if—and this happens regularly—you are so unhappily stopped out that you leave the market at exactly the lowest point, it is still better than being unhappy when the market collapses. You can find a new entry at any time. A new beginning, on the other hand, is unlikely.

We have thus discussed almost all the components you need for the professional planning of a trade under risk aspects. Let us now summarize our prepared individual considerations and use them to determine how much capital you want to, can, or may use for a trade.

Everything on one card? This is how you determine your optimal position size!

In addition to defining the risk to be taken, determining the optimal position size is one of the most important elements of risk management.

Unfortunately, many traders are unaware of this and take a too large position in relation to their trading account. You are unknowingly taking a greater risk than you originally planned. For this reason, the professional determination of the optimal position size is the decisive factor in risk management and at the same time, is the link between our planned risk and the stop loss.

You might think: *Wait a minute; with the risk, I have already set everything and with the stop loss I know when I will exit the trade. What the h*** is this now?!* In fact, it is precisely this consideration that distinguishes successful traders from the others. After all, with the same system, strategy, and conditions, it is the position size that determines whether a green or a red number appears at the end of your trading statement. Therefore, let us compare different ways of determining the size of the position to find the best one for you.

There are several possibilities for determining the optimal position size. The simplest is, of course, to put everything on one card and fill the trading account completely with one stock. We have already discussed several reasons why this is usually not a good idea.

Another way to make trader life easy is to always buy the same number of units of a share. Especially if you only trade a handful of markets regularly, this habit creeps in quickly. For example, if you trade forex, this can mean that you always trade 50,000 EUR against 50,000 USD.[4] You may even have this amount already fixed in your trading platform and, regardless of your previous considerations, you will always trade this amount. Or you can trade exclusively the XY-Inc. share and always move 100 shares in the market. No matter what the share price is, there are always 100 shares.

Let's take a look at the example. We remain with our accepted trading account of $10,000. As a risk, we do not want to exceed 1% of our trading account. The stop loss is set by us from a technical point of view and remains in the market until it is either triggered or we sell at a profit. We want to make it easy for ourselves and always buy 10 shares of XY-Inc. That should somehow be possible with our risk

---

[4]   In foreign exchange or Forex trading, trading is on margin. In order to trade 50,000 EUR against 50,000 USD a significantly lower margin deposit is required from your broker than is actually traded in the market.

management. We carry out ten trades and can look back on five winners and five losers afterwards.

The results are shown in the following table:

Pos	Entry	Stop loss	Points until stop loss	Shares	Risk	Positionsize	Exit	Points	Sum	Account
										$10,000.00
1	100	85	15	10	$150.00	$1,000.00	85	-15	-$150.00	$9,850.00
2	110	100	10	10	$100.00	$1,100.00	125	15	$150.00	$10,000.00
3	140	120	20	10	$200.00	$1,400.00	120	-20	-$200.00	$9,800.00
4	120	105	15	10	$150.00	$1,200.00	105	-15	-$150.00	$9,650.00
5	135	115	20	10	$200.00	$1,350.00	165	30	$300.00	$9,950.00
6	160	145	15	10	$150.00	$1,600.00	185	25	$250.00	$10,200.00
7	185	175	10	10	$100.00	$1,850.00	175	-10	-$100.00	$10,100.00
8	185	170	15	10	$150.00	$1,850.00	205	20	$200.00	$10,300.00
9	95	90	5	10	$50.00	$950.00	103	8	$80.00	$10,380.00
10	110	100	10	10	$100.00	$1,100.00	100	-10	-$100.00	$10,280.00
										$10,280.00

Figure 13: The results of 10 trades in a row, arbitrary allocation of winners and losers. The number of shares traded always remains constant.

We can see in Figure 13 that we have achieved a positive overall result. This is the good news that comes with a big BUT. Because if we go into the details, the dangers of this blanket approach come to light. We had assumed that we would constantly buy 10 shares of XY-Inc. and determine the stop loss according to technical criteria. This results in stop loss points, which can be further away from the entry, but also closer. Accordingly, the risk varies sometimes close to our expectations and sometimes not. So, there are positions where we take half of our planned risk and there are positions where it is then again doubled.

Risk and Money Management for Day and Swing Trading

This cannot be optimal and of course it is not. This becomes particularly clear when we have only four winners instead of five.

Let us assume, for example, that trade number eight is not a winner, but a loser. What would the result look like then?

Pos	Entry	Stop loss	Points until stop loss	Shares	Risk	Positionsize	Exit	Points	Sum	Account
										$10,000.00
1	100	85	15	10	$150.00	$1,000.00	85	-15	-$150.00	$9,850.00
2	110	100	10	10	$100.00	$1,100.00	125	15	$150.00	$10,000.00
3	140	120	20	10	$200.00	$1,400.00	120	-20	-$200.00	$9,800.00
4	120	105	15	10	$150.00	$1,200.00	105	-15	-$150.00	$9,650.00
5	135	115	20	10	$200.00	$1,350.00	165	30	$300.00	$9,950.00
6	160	145	15	10	$150.00	$1,600.00	185	25	$250.00	$10,200.00
7	185	175	10	10	$100.00	$1,850.00	175	-10	-$100.00	$10,100.00
8	185	170	15	10	$150.00	$1,850.00	170	-15	-$150.00	$9,950.00
9	95	90	5	10	$50.00	$950.00	103	8	$80.00	$10,030.00
10	110	100	10	10	$100.00	$1,100.00	100	-10	-$100.00	$9,930.00
										$9,930.00

Figure 14: The results deteriorate significantly if the trade number eight becomes a losing trade instead of a winning trade.

If we take one of the bigger winners out of the result and turn it into a loser, the hand turns. That's no surprise. Not only do we lack profit here, we also lose. On top of that, we end up with an overall loss and have to complain about a negative portfolio value.

What does the result look like if we achieve a neutral result instead of a loss with trade number eight—i.e., dissolve the "break-even" position?

Pos	Entry	Stop loss	Points until stop loss	Shares	Risk	Positionsize	Exit	Points	Sum	Account
										$10,000.00
1	100	85	15	10	$150.00	$1,000.00	85	-15	-$150.00	$9,850.00
2	110	100	10	10	$100.00	$1,100.00	125	15	$150.00	$10,000.00
3	140	120	20	10	$200.00	$1,400.00	120	-20	-$200.00	$9,800.00
4	120	105	15	10	$150.00	$1,200.00	105	-15	-$150.00	$9,650.00
5	135	115	20	10	$200.00	$1,350.00	165	30	$300.00	$9,950.00
6	160	145	15	10	$150.00	$1,600.00	185	25	$250.00	$10,200.00
7	185	175	10	10	$100.00	$1,850.00	175	-10	-$100.00	$10,100.00
8	185	170	15	10	$150.00	$1,850.00	205	0	$0.00	$10,100.00
9	95	90	5	10	$50.00	$950.00	103	8	$80.00	$10,180.00
10	110	100	10	10	$100.00	$1,100.00	100	-10	-$100.00	$10,080.00
										$10,080.00

Figure 15: With a neutral result for trade number eight, we will at least return to profitability.

Instead of taking a loss, we may exit a trade with zero. Many traders do this when the profit was already in the books, but the market suddenly lost momentum before the profit could be protected. In this situation many traders are looking for an exit before the former potential winner becomes a real loser.

We see that the results are rather modest. Of course, the distribution of winners and losers is purely arbitrary. But that is exactly what we experience every day in trading. And you must get the best out of these arbitrary conditions!

All in all, the strategy of fixed quantities can be profitable as long as we generate winners in the majority of cases. However, as soon as we experience losses in the majority, this strategy can quickly generate disproportionate losses. This is particularly due to the fact that the risk per position varies. As a result, we are closer to gambling than to professional trading with this approach. The particular danger with

Risk and Money Management for Day and Swing Trading

this approach is that we have to take a too-high risk if the stop loss is too far away. A loss associated with this can then quickly put us in a state of failure. Another point to be criticized with regard to the fixed number of units is the lack of flexibility with regard to changes in the trading account.

So, we know that a fixed number of pieces produces rather moderate results. Perhaps it would be better if we varied the number of pieces and instead always bought our titles for the same amount, so that we always choose the same position size. The risk is thus effectively limited to the amount invested.

Let us assume again by way of example that we always put 10% of our trading account of $10,000 into one position. So, we always buy shares of XY-Inc. with a value of $1,000. However, as there are no half shares, we round down.

How are the results with approximately the same position size?

Pos	Entry	Stop loss	Points until stop loss	Shares	Risk	Positionsize	Exit	Points	Sum	Account
										$10,000.00
1	100	85	15	10	$150.00	$1,000.00	85	-15	-$150.00	$9,850.00
2	110	100	10	9	$90.00	$990.00	125	15	$135.00	$9,985.00
3	140	120	20	7	$140.00	$980.00	120	-20	-$140.00	$9,845.00
4	120	105	15	8	$120.00	$960.00	105	-15	-$120.00	$9,725.00
5	135	115	20	7	$140.00	$945.00	165	30	$210.00	$9,935.00
6	160	145	15	6	$90.00	$960.00	185	25	$150.00	$10,085.00
7	185	175	10	5	$50.00	$925.00	175	-10	-$50.00	$10,035.00
8	185	170	15	5	$75.00	$925.00	205	20	$100.00	$10,135.00
9	95	90	5	10	$50.00	$950.00	103	8	$80.00	$10,215.00
10	110	100	10	9	$90.00	$990.00	100	-10	-$90.00	$10,125.00
										$10,125.00

Figure 16: After 10 trades in a row and 5 winners and 5 losers we have a positive result here as well.

We left the entry, stop loss, and exit unchanged and only fixed the position size. The size of the position then changes not only the number of shares purchased, but also the associated risk per position. Also, here we are regularly above and below our desired value of 1%. As a result, we take disproportionately high risks on the one hand and make disproportionately low use of our opportunities on the other. We can see that the overall result remains below the fixed number of units, which is partly due to the reduced number of units per trade.

What would the results look like if we were to declare trade number eight the loser here as well?

Pos	Entry	Stop loss	Points until stop loss	Shares	Risk	Positionsize	Exit	Points	Sum	Account
										$10,000.00
1	100	85	15	10	$150.00	$1,000.00	85	-15	-$150.00	$9,850.00
2	110	100	10	9	$90.00	$990.00	125	15	$135.00	$9,985.00
3	140	120	20	7	$140.00	$980.00	120	-20	-$140.00	$9,845.00
4	120	105	15	8	$120.00	$960.00	105	-15	-$120.00	$9,725.00
5	135	115	20	7	$140.00	$945.00	165	30	$210.00	$9,935.00
6	160	145	15	6	$90.00	$960.00	185	25	$150.00	$10,085.00
7	185	175	10	5	$50.00	$925.00	175	-10	-$50.00	$10,035.00
8	185	170	15	5	$75.00	$925.00	170	-15	-$75.00	$9,960.00
9	95	90	5	10	$50.00	$950.00	103	8	$80.00	$10,040.00
10	110	100	10	9	$90.00	$990.00	100	-10	-$90.00	$9,950.00
										$9,950.00

Figure 17: With trade number eight on the losing side, the overall result is also negative.

The overall result is only marginally better than the fixed number, but we are still making a loss with our trading account. Here, too, we are behind the possibilities offered by an optimal position size.

Risk and Money Management for Day and Swing Trading

Finally, we can look at what the overall result would be if we were to exit at zero with trade number eight.

Pos	Entry	Stop loss	Points until stop loss	Shares	Risk	Positionsize	Exit	Points	Sum	Account
										$10,000.00
1	100	85	15	10	$150.00	$1,000.00	85	-15	-$150.00	$9,850.00
2	110	100	10	9	$90.00	$990.00	125	15	$135.00	$9,985.00
3	140	120	20	7	$140.00	$980.00	120	-20	-$140.00	$9,845.00
4	120	105	15	8	$120.00	$960.00	105	-15	-$120.00	$9,725.00
5	135	115	20	7	$140.00	$945.00	165	30	$210.00	$9,935.00
6	160	145	15	6	$90.00	$960.00	185	25	$150.00	$10,085.00
7	185	175	10	5	$50.00	$925.00	175	-10	-$50.00	$10,035.00
8	185	170	15	5	$75.00	$925.00	185	0	$0.00	$10,035.00
9	95	90	5	10	$50.00	$950.00	103	8	$80.00	$10,115.00
10	110	100	10	9	$90.00	$990.00	100	-10	-$90.00	$10,025.00
										$10,025.00

Figure 18: Even with a fixed position size, the break-even trade brings a positive overall result.

With the break-even trade, the overall result is positive, but there is no real increase in value.

Fortunately, we have a third way to determine the optimal position size. Where we kept the number of pieces in the first attempt and the position size constant in the second, we try the idea of keeping the risk constant in the third. Maybe this will bring us better results.

So, let's assume again that we want to take exactly 1% risk per trade based on our $10,000 trading account. That is $100 risk, which we accept per position. What do the results look like under otherwise unchanged parameters?

Pos	Entry	Stop loss	Points until stop loss	Shares	Risk	Positionsize	Exit	Points	Sum	Account
										$10,000.00
1	100	85	15	6	$90.00	$600.00	85	-15	-$90.00	$9,910.00
2	110	100	10	10	$100.00	$1,100.00	125	15	$150.00	$10,060.00
3	140	120	20	5	$100.00	$700.00	120	-20	-$100.00	$9,960.00
4	120	105	15	6	$90.00	$720.00	105	-15	-$90.00	$9,870.00
5	135	115	20	5	$100.00	$675.00	165	30	$150.00	$10,020.00
6	160	145	15	6	$90.00	$960.00	185	25	$150.00	$10,170.00
7	185	175	10	10	$100.00	$1,850.00	175	-10	-$100.00	$10,070.00
8	185	170	15	6	$90.00	$1,110.00	205	20	$120.00	$10,190.00
9	95	90	5	20	$100.00	$1,900.00	103	8	$160.00	$10,350.00
10	110	100	10	10	$100.00	$1,100.00	100	-10	-$100.00	$10,250.00
										$10,250.00

Figure 19: The "fixed risk" variant also produces a positive overall result.

Here, too, we are seeing a positive result, which in itself is not too bad. Let's read between the lines. Under what circumstances did this result come about? We have kept our position risk almost constant in each individual trade. As there are no half shares, we were again forced to round off and reduce our risk somewhat. As a result of the constant risk, both the respective number of units and the respective position size vary.

By fixing the risk, we get exactly what we need for our trading. A high number of pieces when the stop loss is close to the entry and a low number of pieces when the stop loss is further away. Since the risk always remains the same, we thus preserve the opportunity for high profits through the corresponding variable number of shares.

What will the result look like now if we turn the eighth trade into a loser again?

Risk and Money Management for Day and Swing Trading

Pos	Entry	Stop loss	Points until stop loss	Shares	Risk	Positionsize	Exit	Points	Sum	Account
										$10,000.00
1	100	85	15	6	$90.00	$600.00	85	-15	-$90.00	$9,910.00
2	110	100	10	10	$100.00	$1,100.00	125	15	$150.00	$10,060.00
3	140	120	20	5	$100.00	$700.00	120	-20	-$100.00	$9,960.00
4	120	105	15	6	$90.00	$720.00	105	-15	-$90.00	$9,870.00
5	135	115	20	5	$100.00	$675.00	165	30	$150.00	$10,020.00
6	160	145	15	6	$90.00	$960.00	185	25	$150.00	$10,170.00
7	185	175	10	10	$100.00	$1,850.00	175	-10	-$100.00	$10,070.00
8	185	170	15	6	$90.00	$1,110.00	170	-15	-$90.00	$9,980.00
9	95	90	5	20	$100.00	$1,900.00	103	8	$160.00	$10,140.00
10	110	100	10	10	$100.00	$1,100.00	100	-10	-$100.00	$10,040.00
										$10,040.00

Figure 20: Again, the eighth trade is a loser, but the overall result remains positive!

There you go; right now it pays off to keep the risk constant. Then it does not matter whether the stop loss is further or closer to the entry point. And that's why with good money management—please be patient until then—positive results are achieved even if we have less than 50% success. In this case we even come to a positive overall result with a success rate of only 40%!

Finally, let's take a look at the result that occurs when trade number eight is a break-even trade.

Pos	Entry	Stop loss	Points until stop loss	Shares	Risk	Positionsize	Exit	Points	Sum	Account
										$10,000.00
1	100	85	15	6	$90.00	$600.00	85	-15	-$90.00	$9,910.00
2	110	100	10	10	$100.00	$1,100.00	125	15	$150.00	$10,060.00
3	140	120	20	5	$100.00	$700.00	120	-20	-$100.00	$9,960.00
4	120	105	15	6	$90.00	$720.00	105	-15	-$90.00	$9,870.00
5	135	115	20	5	$100.00	$675.00	165	30	$150.00	$10,020.00
6	160	145	15	6	$90.00	$960.00	185	25	$150.00	$10,170.00
7	185	175	10	10	$100.00	$1,850.00	175	-10	-$100.00	$10,070.00
8	185	170	15	6	$90.00	$1,110.00	185	0	$0.00	$10,070.00
9	95	90	5	20	$100.00	$1,900.00	103	8	$160.00	$10,230.00
10	110	100	10	10	$100.00	$1,100.00	100	-10	-$100.00	$10,130.00
										$10,130.00

Figure 21: As expected, the overall result is positive even with the break-even trade.

Of course, the result remains positive now, just as in the two previous versions of the analysis.

We can still deepen the idea of fixed risk. In our variant we have practically frozen the risk at the initial amount of our trading account. Within a certain account size, this makes perfect sense, since small subtleties in the cent range cannot be reproduced, especially with stocks, due to the lack of the ability to denominate shares. Of course, the situation is different as the account grows. Then it is advisable not to select the original account size as the reference point, but always the current one. This further reinforces the advantage of constant risk, which is why we prefer to speak of "fixed percentage risk."

We have already noticed when determining the risk that we have an automatic brake in the event of a loss, since with a smaller account the

Risk and Money Management for Day and Swing Trading

absolute amount at risk and thus the position size becomes smaller. The only thing that remains the same is the percentage risk.

This allows us to grow quickly in good times with several profits in a row and to slowly save our account in bad times. We have this automatic effect of brake and accelerator pedal neither with the fixed quantity nor with the fixed position size. This is also the reason why these two variants regularly lead to suboptimal results. We will look at this effect again in the last chapter of this book.

So, make use of the fixed percentage risk methodology and professionalize your risk management!

How do Rick, Anna and Peter take our findings and implement them in their trading practice? Let's hear what Rick has to say:

The stop loss makes perfect sense to me. Especially since I enter the market in forex trading with a lever, it is important for me to limit my risk accordingly. The best way to do this is via technical analysis. Actually, I always wanted to trade fixed amounts of $10,000, but of course, fixing the risk makes more sense. Fortunately, my broker also allows me to trade very small denominations via mini- and micro-lots, so that I can always work with the same risk percentage.

With Rick, two points come together that we need to explain in more detail. On the one hand Rick has "only" $5,000 on his trading account, but trades amounts of $10,000 or higher. This is made possible by the fact that forex trading is not carried out in a ratio of 1:1, but "leveraged" in a ratio of 1:100 or higher. This theoretically allows Rick to trade 100 times his stake. Especially if you are acting in a leveraged manner, prudent risk management is a top priority for you.

On the other hand, Rick speaks of mini- and micro-lots. Many brokers offer small and very small denominations in forex trading, which makes it possible to precisely match risk management and position size. This allows you to work professionally even with a relatively small account.

What are Anna's thoughts? How does she approach the determination of the optimal position size?

Since I mainly want to trade stocks or ETFs on analysis of the weekly chart in the longer term, the stop loss will regularly be far from my entry. This will probably allow me to buy only a few pieces of a stock. On the other hand, this also allows me to place several stocks and companies in my portfolio, which gives me a broader spread. Since I trade defensively, I will round down when determining my position size.

Anna raises another interesting point here. By purchasing smaller position sizes due to the more distant stops, she has the opportunity to add more different stocks to her portfolio and thus increase the chances of profits. It goes without saying that she must then pay particular attention to her overall risk.

Finally, let's listen to Peter. What are his thoughts?

With me it's relatively simple. Of course, I will carry out my technical analysis according to all rules of the art. I prefer to place the stop loss a little further away from my entry so that I don't get stopped out unhappily. After all, I want to give the market a chance to breathe. This also determines my position size, which I enter per position.

A brief summary of the most important facts:

> > Risk management helps you to get rid of "performance killers" in time and to maintain your financial basis.

> > In reality, the way back becomes an almost unsolvable task when large disproportionate losses occur. From a loss of 50%, a gain of 100% must be achieved in order to return to the starting point. In order to always remain capable of action, it is important for you to determine a risk amount per position that is mentally and financially bearable for you. This amount is determined depending on your trading account and regularly varies between 1% and 2% of your trading account. In addition to the individual risk, it is also important to set an amount that will limit your overall risk. At the same time, you should set up a plan indicating what to do when this amount is reached. To protect your trades against disproportionate losses, it is necessary to set a point at which the probability of success

is no longer given. This point is your stop loss. In practice, the stop loss is determined by means of technical chart marks and is ideally entered into the market when the position is opened.

> The optimal position size can be determined via the stop loss and the risk taken per trade. The percentage risk is fixed depending on the trading account and the number of units to be traded while the amount of capital to be used varies from position to position.

CHAPTER 3:
Money Management

A well-known trading rule says: "Limit your losses, let profits run." This well-intentioned rule is especially given to newcomers to the markets. But is it really advisable to always proceed this way?

In practice, in extreme cases, we have to imagine that traders open a position, place their stop loss in the market and then let the trade run. They often do not have a concrete goal for their trade. The winnings are left to chance.

Can we really call such an approach professional trading?

It is undisputed that a trade needs "air to breathe" and freedom of movement after its opening. But to let a trade go just like that?

In order for profits to run successfully, we need a trend that brings only minor corrections. It is precisely at this point that theory meets practice: how often and how long do we have such trends compared to upward and downward limited sideways movements?

For this reason, we must critically examine this traditional trading rule. What happens if you follow this rule in a sideways market? You will regularly return your initial book profits as the market moves back and forth between its limits.

Often this strategy resembles a game of chance and the outcome is uncertain. When a trade does work out and a high profit is generated, the joy is great. On the other hand, however, there is a large number of trades that have been stopped somewhere between a small profit, break-even, or a loss. In sum, we can quickly say: "Nothing has been done except for expenses." What pleases the broker is all the more annoying for the dedicated trader.

In addition to the unrealized gains, there is another point. Imagine investing your time in technical analysis, identifying an interesting stock, and opening a position according to your strategy. Your trading idea works out and you see how the book profit increases steadily. Since you want to let the profit run, you give the trade room. And there comes what must come—the momentum is weakening, the price is beginning to fall, and what was previously a respectable book profit is melting together like butter in the sun.

Imagine this scenario not only once, but in—let's say—about one third of your executed trades. Now ask yourself:

> How much can you still trust your trading strategy?
> How much can you trust yourself and your analytical work?
> How safely do you want to hold on to trading?
> With what expectation do you open the next trade?

What remains is frustration. About the time invested, the lost profits, and the changing emotions. It is no longer helpful if every now and then a really good trade with a high profit finds its way into your statistics. The frustration with the many situations where the profit was already tangible and has disappeared into nothingness will simply be too great to build a stable trust in yourself and your trading strategy.

Ultimately, such an approach will end up in you constantly hoping for the big winner to compensate you for the efforts of the many small failures. In this context, it is quickly said: "If I had joined the XY share at that time, everything would be fine now. . . ." The question that inevitably follows is: "And when exactly did you want to get out of this big winner?"

One final point completes our critical discussion. At the beginning of the book, you asked yourself what you wanted to achieve with your trading. Do you remember? Good. At this point, let us assume that you want to earn money with your trading.

Ask yourself, "Do you want to leave this to chance or achieve it by continuous profits?"

At this point, we leave risk management and take the first steps towards professional money management by considering concrete profit targets and target achievement.

From risk management to money management: What does risk limitation have to do with determining profits?

As part of our risk limiting process, we had determined that trading is based on probabilities and entered our stop loss at that point in the chart where the probability of our trading idea working out no longer exists. By putting a stop to disproportionate losses and orienting ourselves towards probabilities, we have been able to gain security for the implementation of our trading decisions.

When it comes to profits, we face the same situation. Simply letting the profits go means, in turn, entering uncertainty. We have already established that you cannot predict the future. Just as you don't know in *which* direction the price will actually move after you have entered the market, you don't know *how far* the price will move in that direction.

To turn this further aspect of uncertainty into certainty as well, we can again apply the concept of probabilities. We use technical analysis to identify the point which the price is most likely to reach.

As a rule of thumb, we can say that the nearest points are the most likely ones to be reached. The further away a target is from the entry, the lower the probability that it will be reached in the foreseeable future without correction.

For your trade planning, this means that you can expect to achieve targets quickly if they are close at hand, and you must plan for corrections if they are further away.

There are several methods for determining the profit target. Let us take a closer look at two of them. One here and the other in the next section.

You will recall that we used the last low after a correction in the beginning trend to determine our stop loss. We follow a similar path for the determination of profits.

For our profit target, we are looking for a point that can be reached with a high degree of probability within the current movement. This is usually the last high after a correction or the nearest resistance in the trend. Since we can expect a counter-reaction at these points on a regular basis, it makes sense for you to set your profit target here.

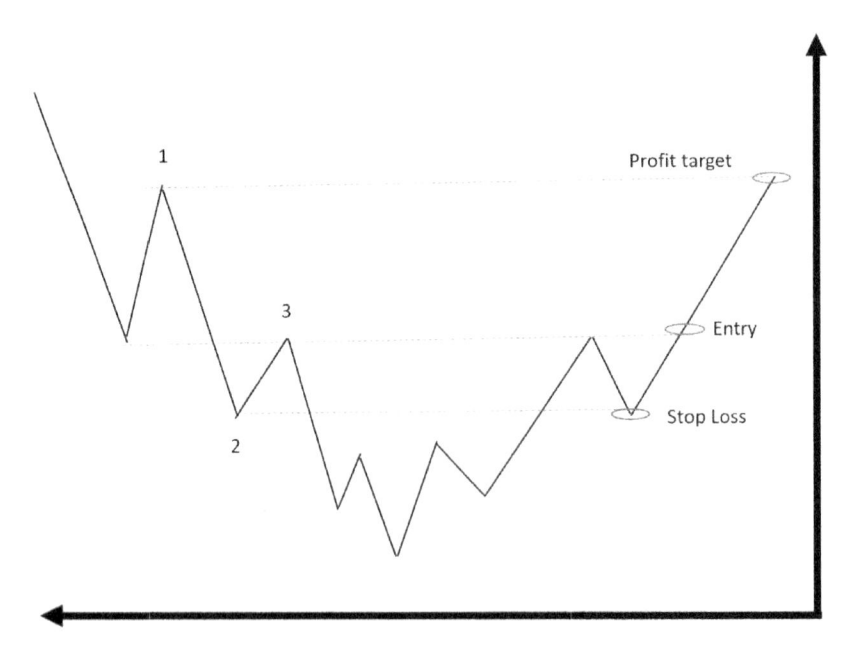

Figure 22: Definition of a profit target in an uptrend.

Figure 22 shows us the typical course of any market with a downtrend, a bottom formation and a trend reversal. With the peak reached at point 1 and the follow-up correction to the support at point 2, we can assume that there is buying interest among market participants.

We want to open the position when the price breaks through the resistance at point 3. We place the stop loss below the last low at point 2, where we simultaneously identified a support. As we enter a new trend and speculate that a new high will be reached, we choose the next resistance within reach as our target, which is at point 1. At this point we can expect at least a temporary correction. To secure our profit, we exit the trade at this point.

We want to get out of the uncertainty and also gain certainty for the case of profit. Even at the risk of slaughtering one of the holy trading cows at this point, there can therefore only be one recommendation:

Set yourself a concrete profit target and take your winnings there!

We can transfer this procedure directly into practice and look at the GBP/USD currency pair:

Figure 23: GBP/USD, daily chart (one candle = one day). After a decline, the currency pair is forming a bottom and is beginning to form a new uptrend. Source: www.tradingview.com

The GBP/USD currency pair has found a bottom at USD 1.19583 after a sell-off to point 1. There the currency pair stabilizes and climbs to the resistance line at USD 1.25344—our point 2. As expected, the currency pair falls back from there and forms a higher low at point 3. As you already know, this indicates at least temporary buying interest, which we want to use for a trade. We place our entry just above point 2 at USD 1.25367. We set our stop loss below point 3 at USD 1.2190. As a target, we are targeting the area that has formed a relevant resistance in the past: the range between USD 1.29755 and USD 1.33281. There we want to exit our trade at a profit.

Now you may ask yourself why this particular point was chosen. There are several reasons for this. On the one hand, you can see that at point B the price rebounded two times downwards with a support at Point A. These points limit a zone in which the prices range for a couple of days, so we can see them as a potential resistance area. In the USD 1.29755 area—where the support at point A is located—there have been several reactions. An undershooting of the support was not permanent. For this reason, the line at point A should build a high probability resistance. Therefore, the chances are high that the price rebounds there. In order to keep the profits, we will exit here with a part—i.e., the half—of the position. On the other hand, the area around the round number is considered particularly reactive, especially in forex trading. These areas, such as USD 1.33000, are under particular observation by many market participants. In that area is also the resistance line at Point B, where buyers already failed. Also, for this reason, it is advisable to exit the other part of the position there to secure the accrued profits.

As we continue, we can see that we were able to take almost the entire stretch of the upmove after the breakout. What also emerges is that following our exit, a consolidation has formed that offered at least two more interesting trading opportunities at the new-found support.

If you compare these observations with the "let profits run" alternative, where do you see the better opportunities for you to make money and increase your trading capital?

Through your successful trades you can also build your confidence as a trader. Contrast this to the trader who has experienced several times during this movement that his book profit regularly melts down and as a result, slowly starts to doubt himself and his strategy.

For the technical implementation of your strategy, in most trading platforms, you can enter your price target simultaneously with your stop loss order and place it in the market.[5] In this way your two "boundary posts" are set and you know the full outcome of your trade with certainty when you open a position.

Now we have put together all the components you need to get certainty into your trading. You know when opening a position what you can lose at most and you also know what you can win at best. But what you don't know yet is whether a trade really makes sense, or whether you should rather wait for another opportunity. Let's settle this now.

Chance or risk? How to improve the quality of your trades!

One of the most important components for lasting success in trading is the ability to separate promising opportunities from the unpromising ones and only enter into trades that have a corresponding profit potential.

Unfortunately, you don't know this beforehand and you have to use the concept of probabilities to find at least some certainty. As discussed above, you need to set a profit target which can be achieved with a high probability for each trade. Of course, it makes no sense to choose a target that is close to entry just to make a quick profit. If you proceeded in this way, you would have many small profits, which could be eliminated by one loss. This calculation cannot, of course, work out in the long term.

---

[5] This then happens as a so-called OCO order: One-Cancels-Other. If one order is triggered, the other is automatically deleted. This is to ensure that no open orders from you remain in the market by mistake.

Risk and Money Management for Day and Swing Trading

For this reason, it is important that you compare the potential loss and potential gain of a trade. Always know what you want and need to be adequately compensated for the risk you have taken on your investment.

This ratio is indicated by the risk/reward ratio. The risk/reward ratio—RRR for short—indicates how high the profit is in relation to the risk taken. The calculation is very simple:

$$RRR = \frac{Win}{Loss}$$

For example, if we plan a trade where we can make a profit of $100 and our defined risk is $50, then our risk/reward ratio is

$$RRR = \frac{\$100}{\$50} = 2$$

Assuming we would be satisfied with a small profit of $50, our risk/reward ratio would look like this:

$$RRR = \frac{\$50}{\$50} = 1$$

As a final scenario for this, we can look at what the risk/reward ratio looks like if we exit with a small profit of—let's say—$25 if we close our trade immediately after opening and making the first profits:

$$RRR = \frac{\$25}{\$50} = 0.5$$

From the risk/reward ratio you can see when a trade makes sense and when it does not. It's like any investment: If we know from the beginning that we will get less than we risk, then this investment makes no sense. The risk/reward ratio expresses this logic in figures.

For interpretation, this means that the minimum requirement you must have for your risk/reward ratio is RRR = 1. If the risk/reward ratio is less than 1, you are taking a higher risk than the trade promises as a profit. In addition to this, you calculate with probabilities for the winning case, so it is not certain whether the profit is actually in this amount. In the event of a loss, you also calculate probabilities, but if this occurs, then you know with absolute certainty what you can lose. This built-in disadvantage further reinforces the too-low risk/reward ratio to your disadvantage.[6]

Accordingly, the minimum requirement for the risk/reward ratio must be 1. Then you will be paid the same amount for the risk you have taken. In the event of a loss, a previous profit is immediately erased. All in all, you have to be very successful to achieve significant results with this risk/reward ratio.

Obviously, it is then better to choose a risk/reward ratio that is significantly higher. In practice, a value of 1.5 to 2 has proven to be practicable. An RRR = 1.5 means that you will receive 1.5 times the risk you took if you succeed. An example:

Assuming you make two trades, one of which is a winner and the other a loser, you have made a total gain equal to half your risk. Especially since you assume that you have to expect losses in trading on a regular basis and explicitly plan for them, this approach makes sense.

For the planning and execution of your trades, this means that you omit those trades where it is obvious from the beginning that the chance of winning is less than the risk taken. From a risk/reward perspective, these simply do not make sense. A loss throws you further back than a gain would advance you.

Before we critically discuss the risk/reward ratio, let's take a look at the risk/reward ratio we have planned for our trade in GBP/USD:

---

[6] In fact, there are a number of drawbacks that you have to overcome on every single trade. These are the already mentioned fees, the spread, and also a possible slippage. You have to make up for all of these points on your way to winning before you are really in the profit.

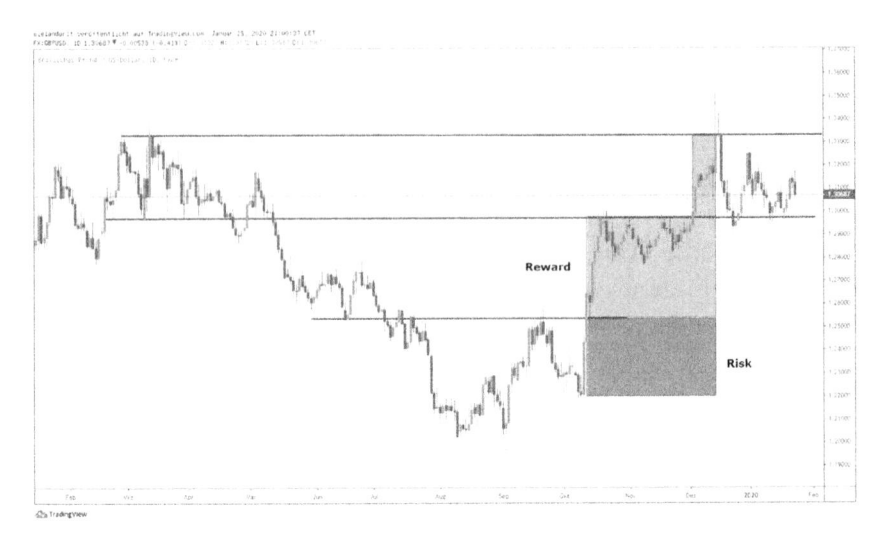

Risk and Money Management for Day and Swing Trading

Figure 24: GBP/USD, daily chart (one candle = one day). The risk/reward ratio is marked in our trade and just by visual inspection you can see that the RRR is > 1. Source: www.tradingview.com

We had planned our trade with an entry at USD 1.25367, a stop loss at USD 1.21900 and a target at USD 1.29755 and/or USD 1.33000. What is the risk/reward ratio?

The risk is:

$$Entry - Stop\ Loss = Risk$$
$$USD\ 1.25367 - USD\ 1,21900 = 3,467 = 346.7\ Pips^7$$

The planned profit amounts to:

$$Target - Entry = Profit$$
$$USD\ 1.29755 - USD\ 1.25367 = 4,388 = 438.8\ Pips$$

---

[7] A pip in forex trading is the fourth decimal place. A change of one pip represents a change of one. For example, from USD 1.25360 to USD 1.25370.

The risk/reward profile is as follows:

$$RRR = \frac{4{,}388}{3{,}467} = 1.27$$

We see that the RRR is >1. This means that the trade is basically feasible. If we include the costs of a trade such as fees, spread,[8] and possibly a worse-than-planned execution—the so-called slippage[9]—the risk/reward ratio deteriorates even further. The trade is therefore still feasible, but a risk/reward ratio of this amount should not be the rule.

Let us take up another point in this context. At this point please think back to our calculation of the optimal position size. There we only had four winners out of ten trades. Nevertheless, we were still able to achieve a positive result, assuming a constant percentage risk. The reason was that the winning trades were larger than the losing trades. The risk/reward ratio was significantly above 1 in each case.

For you this means that you do not always have to be right with your analysis. You do not have to close every trade with a profit to achieve positive overall results. Your winners just have to be bigger than your losers. That's the whole secret. What sounds so simple in theory is known to be much more difficult in practice. For this reason, it is also right and important to set a concrete target that can be achieved with a high degree of probability in order to end the trade at this point.

The further away the target is from your entry, the less likely it is to be reached in a reasonable time and without significant corrections. This also means that the probability of achieving a very high risk/reward ratio is also low. The higher the targeted risk/reward ratio should be, the lower the probability that you will achieve it promptly and directly.

---

[8] Spread is the difference between the bid and ask price. As a rule, the bid price is lower than the ask price.

[9] Slippage is defined as an order execution that is worse than the desired order execution. This can occur both when opening and closing a position and, under unfavorable circumstances, can significantly worsen the results.

Here too, we must have a critical discussion. We often hear from traders that they only enter into trades that promise a risk/reward ratio of 3, 4, or 5. How many missed good chances do you think these traders will have to take on their way to the big profit? How realistic is such a statement?

In planning, it is certainly right and important to identify and define large potentials. However, you must also realize your profit at the point where it is most likely to disappear again.

Last but not least, when looking at a trade, it is not only a matter of determining what potential it holds, but also of measuring in retrospect what risk/reward ratio has actually been realized. Only this point is the decisive factor. Only this consideration indicates whether a trader trades successfully or not.

When planning your next trades, it is therefore recommended that you select trades that offer a risk/reward ratio of 1.5 or 2 and are likely to achieve your targets. Then, in retrospect, you will be able to claim exactly these ratios in the total again for yourself.

You probably guessed it already. You can also set your profit target via a fixed risk/reward ratio. For example, if you specify that you always want to realize an RRR = 1.5, then set this as your profit target. Using technical analysis, you should then ensure that the probability of reaching the target is also given.

Finally, a few words about dealing with probabilities. Although we have dealt with what seems likely and what not, we have not considered concrete statistical evidence in this regard. That's not possible, either. In the world of trading there is an infinite number of markets, methods, trading styles, products, and strategies. These can be combined at will and implemented in a wide variety of time frames. A blanket consideration of rigid statistics makes no sense due to this variety of possibilities. In the end, you will have to develop and refine your own strategy and act according to your individual requirements and preferences. If, from your point of view, the achievement of a profit target is rather unlikely, then this is a sure signal for you not to enter the trade or at least to choose another profit target. This does not necessarily mean that another trader does not have the exact opposite opinion to you at the same moment under his personal conditions and strategies based on them. This is important, right, and good. After all, the multitude of market opinions, trading ideas, and individual circumstances is one of the reasons why trading takes place at all in the financial markets.

For this reason, consider the concept of probabilities as a subjective decision-making aid that helps you to carry out your trading according to your personal ideas and individual requirements.

A brief summary of the most important facts:

> In addition to minimizing risk, it is also important for you to make concrete profit-target planning.
> Especially in volatile markets, it makes sense to regularly secure accumulated profits.
> When determining profits, ask yourself: Where is the market most likely to go?
> The risk/reward ratio—RRR—can be calculated using the defined components risk and profit, which indicates the relationship between profit and risk taken.
> Trades with a risk/reward ratio below one have a too-high risk compared to the expected profit and should be avoided.
> You have realistic chances with a risk/reward ratio between one and two.
> The further away the profit target is from the starting price and the higher the planned risk/reward ratio, the lower the probability that the target will be reached in the foreseeable future without corrections. More important than the planned risk/reward ratio is the realized risk/reward ratio for professional performance control.
> With a risk/reward ratio greater than one, you can afford to have more losers without incurring the overall loss.

CHAPTER 4:
Risk and Money Management in Practice

Stocks, Forex and Futures—How to professionally apply risk and money management to your trading account

How can you professionally transfer your risk and money management in the form you are now familiar with into practice? What do you need to pay attention to and what do possible calculations and results look like? Let's visit our three traders and look over their shoulders as they plan their positions.

Let us first visit Rick, our forex trader:

I had already thought about the risk I was taking and I assume that higher price targets are regularly achievable in forex trading. I think there is so much volatility in the forex market, there should always be a good risk/reward ratio for me. On the other hand, I don't want to wait forever to get my profits in either. I want in and out fast. For me, a risk/reward ratio of 1.5 therefore makes sense. I have already studied technical analysis in depth, so I will find many potential winners!

It is good and important to recognize if you want to wait for your success or if you want to access it quickly. Rick has made a clear decision here and has also already emphasized that he wants to act rather aggressively. A risk/reward ratio of 1.5 is high enough to compensate for any losses incurred. If Rick is right with his statement and not only expects the many winners but also achieves them, then on this basis he will make good progress towards his goal. If, on the other hand, the losers are clearly in the majority, then he must reconsider his target figure.

Rick also brought us a trade that he wants to present to us:

Figure 25: AUD/USD, 60-minutes chart (one candle = 60 minutes). The points 1 - 7 mark the respective highs and lows within the trend movement. Point 6 marks the entry level, point 7 is the stop loss and point 8 marks the target of the trade with a RRR = 1.5. The rectangles graphically represent the risk/reward ratio. Source: www.tradingview.com

In my analysis of the AUD/USD, I discovered a good opportunity on the 60-minute chart. I identified a beginning uptrend that was about to establish after forming a double-bottom. At point 1, I found a low, which was followed by a high at point 2. With point 3, a low at the same level as low 1 was formed, which for me was a first sign that there might be a bottom. When a new high was reached with point 4, followed by a higher low at 5 and a steep rise to 6, I decided to take the trade with the break of the last high at point 6. And indeed, a higher low was formed at point 7! With the break out of the high at point 6, my setup was complete and I opened my trade!

My associated planning is as follows:

Rick	Account size	Risk per trade in percent	Risk per trade in USD	Entry	Stop Loss
	$5,000.00	1.0%	$50.00	$0.68833	$0.68610
Risk in Pips	**Position size**	**RRR**	**Profit in Pips**	**Profit target**	**Profit in USD**
$0.00223	$22,421.52	1.5	$0.00354	$0.69188	$79.48

Figure 26: Rick's planning for his trade

Since forex trading is 24 hours a day, I have added a stop buy order to my entry so I don't have to wait until my entry is reached to enter manually. At the same time, I have entered my stop loss and target after the opening, so that I am covered downwards when opening and can take my profits upwards. In my calculations the spread is planned with two pips, which I have added to my target. There are no fees charged by my broker for forex trading, so I don't have to make up for any additional costs. Since forex trading is very liquid, I have not included a slippage in the form of a bad execution.

Based on my risk amount per trade I can go with a risk of $50. If I deduct the price at the stop loss from the entry price, I come to a risk of 22 pips. With my target of an RRR = 1.5 this results in a gain of 33 pips. If I add the spread, it's 35 pips. I add this to the price at my entry and I have already calculated the price at my target. The calculation of my position size is one of those things, though. Since I have a little over $22,000 available as a position size, I am glad that my broker also offers small denominations. With two mini- and two micro-lots, I can place anything up to $421 in the market.

After calculating my target, I looked at the chart to see how likely it is that my target can be achieved. I had to realize that on the way to the finish line there is still a resistance waiting where the recent downtrend made a lower high. Here, at least short-term reaction or a pause in the uptrend is likely. However, I assume that the price will ultimately break through this *resistance, as the downtrend seems to be over. If, contrary to expectations, it does go against my preferred direction, I am covered by the stop loss just in case.*

The trade has been very slow after the opening. Immediately after I was stopped in the trade, things went sideways for a while. As expected, the move up made a small correction in the resistance area, but fortunately it did not really go down. After that the price went up again followed by two more price corrections and went then into my profit target. In hindsight I could also have reached a higher RRR as the price went 10 pips higher after my exit."

If you take a closer look at the implementation of Rick's plan, the consequence for you will be that you will have to round up or down your position size or stake regularly. Although a position size of $22,421 was specified in Rick's planning, he was only able to position $22,000 in the market with mini and micro lots. Although the difference is not earth-shattering, it is reflected in the results. Both the risk taken and the profit achieved are slightly below plan due to the downward adjusted position size. This shows that you must always adapt your calculations to the possibilities of the market and the product. In the course of the trade Rick's patience was put to the test and he had to hold the position through several price corrections. In the end, we see that a moderate RRR of 1.5 also needs to be developed.

How did Anna—our position trader—approach her planning?

Since I tend to take a longer-term view, a price target that is too narrow makes no sense to me. I even think that I want to give myself and my trade a lot of leeway so that I don't have to change positions too often. When I catch a trend, I want to stay with it as long as possible! For this reason, I have decided to set the planned risk/reward ratio at 2.5. This is often within the bounds of what is feasible. But I also know that I will probably have to go through one or two corrections here in order to achieve my target. Nevertheless, I feel good about it and this approach suits me and my attitude. I put a bit more risk into the position, but I also expect a bit more in return.

Anna executes her trades on the weekly chart and thus automatically sets herself to a longer-term time frame. The regular target of achieving a risk/reward ratio of 2.5 is ambitious and ultimately depends on the market and the strength of the trend. Especially when looking at the weekly chart, trends often come into play cleanly and the short-term ups and downs in the daily chart are not even noticeable. With appropriate trade management, Anna can achieve good results with her approach.

Anna also wants to present us a trade and lets us in on her thoughts:

I identified an interesting setup in the Apple (AAPL) weekly chart and made my calculations on it:

Figure 27: APPLE INC (AAPL), weekly chart (one candle = one week). The points 1 - 4 mark the respective highs and lows within the trend movement. Point 5 marks the entry, point 4 is also the stop loss and point 6 marks the profit target of the trade with a RRR = 2.5. The rectangles graphically represent the respective risk/reward ratio. Source: www.tradingview.com

Since October 2016, AAPL has been on a long-term uptrend, moving steadily upwards. After AAPL made a sharp correction from point 1 in October 2018 and reached point 2 two months later, AAPL went up again to point 3 and then back to point 4—a higher low. For me, this was a first sign that I could take a closer look at the stock. When AAPL headed north *again after the price correction to point 4, I decided to use a break through the resistance at point 3 as an entry.*

My calculations accordingly look as follows:

Anna	Account size	Risk per trade in percent	Risk per trade in USD	Entry	Stop Loss
	$25.000	1.50%	$375	$216	$166
Risk per share	**Position size**	**RRR**	**Profit in Pips**	**Profit target**	**Profit in USD**
$50	7.5	2.5	$125	$341	$938

Figure 28: Anna´s calculation

I have decided to take a 1.5% risk on my trading account. That's $375 currently. If I include my entry point at $216 and the stop loss at $166 in my calculations, I can buy seven shares. As there are no half shares, I have to round down.

However, during the chart analysis, I then discovered that my calculated target with an RRR = 2.5 at $341 is a multiple all-time high, so I will certainly have to adjust to several corrections. Especially in the area of the former high and also the round number at $300, the probability of a reaction is very high. Nevertheless, I stand by it. I definitely want to take a stand, not only because I like their products but I also think that Apple still is way ahead of its competitors. I am well covered by my stop loss and can follow it up in my trade management.

As it turns out, AAPL broke through the last high without any hesitation. Although the correction at $300 didn´t happen, the stock went heavily into the direction of my profit target. Although there are still a few dollars missing, I am sure that AAPL will reach my profit target no matter what. To make sure that my gained profits remain in my pockets, I am managing the trade with a tighter trailing stop loss.

What I still have to deduct from my profit are the fees for the entry and the exit. As I am a long-term investor, the spread of €0.02[10] per share is negligible for me.

Anna remains confident and patient throughout the trade. She has carried out her chart analysis conscientiously and strictly limited the risk and secured her profits during the trade. A loss would not throw her off track. So, there's no reason for Anna to be hesitant or to quarrel. As a position trader, she has a longer-time horizon, as can be seen from the duration of the six-month trade. That corrections occur during a holding period of several months is only normal and is part of trading. That they don't happen also occurs from time to time.

Last but not least, Peter would like to discuss his trading idea and his resulting planning with us. What is the planning for our futures trader?

It is important to me to be properly compensated for the risk I have taken. Therefore, a risk/reward ratio of 2.0 is appropriate for me. Then I can get out of the market again and do not run the risk of unhappily running into losses due to adverse circumstances.

Before we proceed, let´s talk about gaps for a while. Traders regularly run the risk of being surprised by a "gap" or "price gap" in overnight positions. For a trader speculating on rising prices, a gap means nothing more than that the opening price in the morning may be significantly lower than the price at the close of the previous day. In this case we speak of a "down gap." For a trader speculating on falling prices, the gap is correspondingly if the morning price is above the previous day's closing price. The synonym for this is then "up gap."

The risk of a price gap is borne by every trader who holds positions overnight. Here, too, the following applies: The more short-term you position yourself, the greater the impact a price gap will have on your risk management. For example, if you plan your trades in a weekly

---

[10] For Anna's entry, the bid price is $216 and the ask price is $216.02. For Anna's exit, the bid price is $341 and the ask price $341.02. Traders buy at the ask price and sell at the bid price.

chart like Anna, you will often not notice any price gaps at all. On the other hand, if you plan your trades like Rick in the 60-minutes chart, then a price gap can have a strong impact on your risk management. You may subsequently exit your position at a significantly worse price because your stop loss order was executed at a significantly lower price than you planned.

Consequently, the existence of price gaps is also a good reason for you to design your risk management defensively and not to exhaust it to the last cent.

Let's get back to Peter. *I like to present a trade in the Gold future. According to my account size, I have chosen the e-Micro, traded at the Comex.*

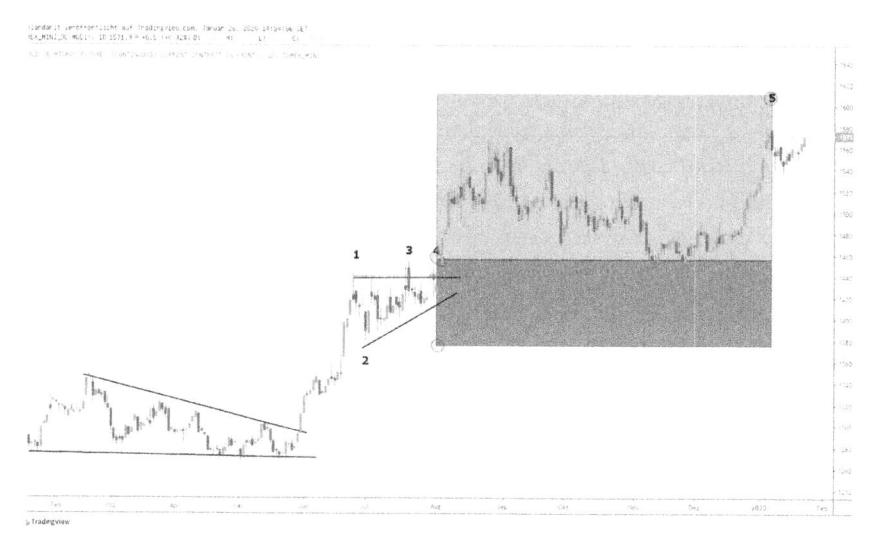

Figure 29: MICRO GOLD FUTURE MGC, daily chart (one candle = one day). The points 1, 3, 4 mark the equal highs forming a resistance and point 2 is the low of the forming a rising triangle. Point 4 marks the entry, point 2 marks the stop loss and point 5 the calculated profit target of the trade. The rectangles graphically represent the respective risk/reward ratio. Source: www.tradingview.com

After a breakout of the falling triangle, gold has risen to point 1 and made a price correction to point 2 after that price reached a more or less equal high at point 3. The following correction didn't go as far as the former one and so did also the next after reaching point 4. All in all, a rising triangle was formed and I had the idea to follow the established trend when price breaks the resistance zone.

Here´s my calculation for my trade:

Peter	Account size	Risk per trade in percent	Risk per trade in USD	Entry	Stop Loss
	$15,000	0.75%	$112.50	$1,455.30	$1,377.40
Risk per lot	**Position size**	**RRR**	**Profit in ticks**	**Profit target**	**Profit in USD**
$77.90	1.44	2	$156	$1,611	$225

Figure 30: Peters planning for his trade in Gold.

In my calculations, I proceeded in such a way that I first looked for the corresponding marks in the chart for my entry, my stop loss and my target. The target was set by my planned risk/reward ratio of two and I could not find any significant resistance on the way to it. If gold continues to stay in its uptrend, then I will probably have to endure a few corrections on the way to the profit target, but I am well protected on the downside. As a result, the points of action were fixed for me. Of course, I could not buy fractions of a future, so I rounded my order down to one. I am better safe than sorry. After the opening of the trade, gold initially went straight up and I thought that it would be a very easy one. But after reaching the area around $1,540 the price went sideways for quite a long time and more than once I saw my entry again. Not the best feeling—I can tell you. But after all, I stood firm and gritted my teeth. Then suddenly after testing the outbreak-zone from the upper side and forming a support the price went up and my profit target has been reached.

After the theoretical conclusions in the previous parts and sections, we were able to follow the ideas in the execution of our three traders in practice. All three traders could report from different experiences. In the case of Rick, he had to go through several price corrections, even though his profit target wasn´t that high. This shows, that a high profit target is reachable when there is high volatility. But if there isn´t, it can take quite a while until price reaches the profit target—as Rick´s experience with his trade.

Anna planned for the long term and has set herself a very high goal with her high risk/reward ratio. In the course of the trade she was pretty lucky, as AAPL went straight and without any price correction towards her profit target. Even though her trade is still running, her tight trade management makes sure that she keeps a big chunk of her accumulated profits.

Peter's experience has shown that you need a good plan and strong nerves to maintain your trade. After a good start he had to go through a sharp correction, which eliminated the book profit gold had made up to that point. At this point, many traders become restless and run the risk of closing their position prematurely. Peter, on the other hand, stuck to his plan and was successful in the end for that very reason. In this sense, a professional planning of a trade is the basic prerequisite to keep your nerves during the execution.

A brief summary of the most important facts:

> Even low planned risk/reward ratios may require more time than planned to be realized.
> Often the calculated position size cannot be placed in the market in full due to a lack of divisibility.
> In order to realize high risk/reward ratios, corrections must be considered. You have to go through these if you want to reach your goal.

PART 2

From being a professional to becoming a top trader

CHAPTER 5:
Risk and Money Management Squared

Actually, you already know everything you need to know to successfully take your first steps in the financial markets. At least when it comes to limiting your risk and securing your profits, no one will ever fool you again. Of course, you can deepen your knowledge of chart technical analysis or learn more about your own personality as a trader. But actually, you already have the tools to become a profitable trader.

Let us take the opportunity to deepen the existing knowledge and take it to the next level. When it comes to money management, it is about more than "just" protecting profits. In essence, money management means just that: managing your money—your available capital. Accordingly, the goal of professional money management must be to combine the influencing factors of your trading in such a way that the best possible results are achieved in the totality of your trades.

You have gotten to know and internalize some of these influencing factors and you are already applying them successfully. Limiting your risk is an essential and fundamental part of this, but also determining the risk/reward ratio of each trade is part of it. With this in mind, we are now finally bringing risk management and money management together.

There are two more points we need to consider first to complete our overall picture. For this purpose, we will leave the consideration of the individual trade and take a closer look at the sum of the trades in an overall period.

The more, the better . . . What influence does the accuracy of your analysis and the number of trades have on your trading success?

We have previously concentrated our considerations on the planning and execution of individual trades. Now in practice you do not just make one trade and then end your trading career. Depending on which trading style you choose, you may have opened and closed several positions in the course of a day. However, you will certainly look back on a large number of trades executed at the end of a month and definitely at the end of a year.

It is only logical that with a total amount of trades, there are not only winners, but also losers on a regular basis. This is perfectly normal and is part of trading. Losses are part of the business; this fact must simply be accepted. In order to get a concrete impression of your results in the medium and long term and also to get exact starting points for your personal improvement of results, I recommend that you keep detailed records of your trading results at this point. Create your own personal trading journal in which you note the most important key points of your trades. These include:

1. Data of the product traded:
    > Name or Symbol of the share, ETF, currency pair or underlying asset in general
    > Direction of the trade: long or short
    > Description of the trading strategy
    > Currency of the asset

2. Initial data:
    > Number of units
    > Date
    > Entry price
    > Position size
    > Fees

3. Planning data:
   - Stop Loss
   - Profit target(s)
   - Planned risk/reward ratio

4. Exit data:
   - Number of units
   - Date
   - Exit price(s)
   - Position Value
   - Fees

5. Evaluation of the trade:
   - Holding period
   - Realized profit/loss per unit
   - Total realized profit/loss
   - Realized risk/reward ratio

6. Total statistics:
   - Total winners
   - Total losers
   - Realized risk/reward ratio overall
   - Number of all trades executed
   - Overall profit/loss

You can extend this list as you wish by adding further points and statistical evaluations that are important for you. For our considerations, however, these points should suffice. From these points alone, you will be able to gain many important insights for your trading. Among other things, you can see in black and white how many winners and losers have found their way into your trading journal within a defined period.

We can put the number of winners and losers within a period of time—for example, a year—in relation to each other for our further consideration. We can determine how high the number of winners in the total number of our trades is. That's the hit rate:

$$\frac{\text{Number of winning trades}}{\text{Number of trades in total}} = \text{Hit rate}$$

The hit rate tells you with which historical probability a trade according to your strategy leads to a profit or becomes a loser. With this statement you get at least a partial insight into the quality of your trades and analysis.

In practice, many traders often concentrate intensively on achieving the highest possible hit rate. This quickly becomes the measure of all things. The higher the better.

How should we judge this? Is the hit rate really the measure of all things?

Suppose you talk to a trader who tells you that he has a 99% hit rate. Out of 100 of his executed trades, 99 trades are winners. Are you talking to a good trader here? An exceptional talent? A master of his profession?

We don't know. We can't. Because in order to judge whether a trader with a high hit rate is a good trader, we have to take a look behind the scenes. The question to be answered in this context is under what circumstances this result was achieved.

Imagine that this trader tells you that he does not practice risk management. *I don't need a stop loss, I have a 99% hit rate.* Or: *The optimal position size for me is the entire account. I have a 99% hit rate.* I'm sure you already see where this is going. Under these circumstances, even one losing trade out of 100 leads to a total loss of the account.

So next time, please ask critically under which circumstances a high hit rate was achieved. Only then will you get the whole picture.

Perhaps you are now asking yourself how high the hit rate must be in order to be able to act successfully. There can be no really definitive answer to this question until we have taken a look at the further circumstances. We can only say this much: Even with a hit rate of less than 50%, you have the chance to become a very successful and highly profitable trader. We have already established this when deriving the optimal position size.

The next point fits this. Assuming you actually have a hit rate that is less than 50%. What do you need to pay particular attention to when selecting and planning your positions? Right. You have to make sure that with each winner you get significantly more out of the market than you would have put into the market with a loser. This is where the risk/reward ratio comes into play again.

Let's use the hit rate to discuss something more fundamental. The hit rate describes the percentage of the winners in the overall result. In the reverse, therefore, also the number of losers.

Let us take a general look at the situation of losing at this point. How about you? Do you like to lose? Can you back down, back off? After a loss, can you just carry on like this right away?

Dealing with losing is not easy for us by nature. We have already discussed this when we were limiting the risks. That is why we introduced the stop loss, so that it would protect us from high losses and thus make our risk predictable and calculable.

What does it generally mean to lose? It does not always have to be about losing a financial amount. Losing is manifold. For example, you can also lose in a discussion—as an example. Or you lose the soccer game already mentioned. We all know how that makes us feel. And we also know that we will do everything we can to avoid losing next time, so that we can be among the winners again.

What is certainly right and important in normal life is the exact opposite in trading. In trading, losses are simply part of the game. They are part of the whole and cannot be avoided. That is why overall performance is always important in trading. A single trade is not decisive with proper management. Neither in one direction nor in the other. Your goal must therefore be to achieve a positive result in the total sum, not in a single trade.

At this point we have to ask ourselves how losses occur in the first place and who is responsible for them. I'm sure there are several reasons. The reasons are to be found on the one hand in the market, but on the other hand also in ourselves. Often in the combination of both.

Let us take a look at a typical situation that occurs every day in countless trading rooms:

Imagine that you have opened your position after professional research and analysis and have placed your stop loss and your profit target into the market. The price moves in your direction; your position seems to be a winner and you see yourself already with the homerun, when suddenly the price turns and slowly but steadily approaches your entry again. The trade threatens to go in the wrong direction and after you have already given away your profit, you don't want to get into the loss as well. Stop loss or not, but that was not the desired outcome. The position is closed quickly and you exit the market at your entry point with "break even." Does this sound familiar to you?

You ended the trade even though neither of your cornerstones was touched. In the end, you threw yourself out of the market. Why? Because nobody likes to lose. Especially not in a row. Ask yourself: what does it mean when you lose in trading? It means nothing else than that you firstly lose money and secondly that you have obviously been wrong in your opinion. So, it's better to pull the rip cord and stop the trade before the loss builds up, isn't it? Getting out without losing your face and money is what we could call this approach.

In this way, a potential winner becomes a secure loser who is also self-inflicted.

Let us go even deeper into this question. Who decides whether your trades are winners or losers? You or the market? Of course, there is just one reasonable answer to this—the market decides the outcome of your trades! Period. But then one question arises: Why do many traders prevent the market from making this decision and choose it arbitrarily by themselves instead?

Remember: After you have opened the position, the market alone calls the shots. Your stop loss provides you with protection against the worst-case scenario and you have already gained security about the outcome. You cannot influence the further direction of the position. You can only let the trade go and manage it properly.

Losing is always connected with the unpleasant question of the responsibility for the loss. Who do you think is responsible for your losses? You, the market, or an anonymous third party? This is also easy to answer. It's always you! The market will not open trades on your behalf and hopefully an anonymous third party will not either. You press the button: Buy! Sell! You must therefore learn to take full responsibility for your trades.

If you did your market and technical analysis to the best of your knowledge and the trade management went according to your trading plan, you do not have to blame yourself if the trade turns into a loser. There's nothing to justify yourself for. Take responsibility for your actions! You just have to admit to yourself that you cannot or must not always be 100% right.

Speaking of personal responsibility: Many traders seek advice in forums, clubs or communities from which they obtain analysis, signals, and strategies for their trading. This approach can be useful in addition to your trading, but of course, it does not allow you to outsource responsibility. Because regardless of who the implemented trading idea ultimately comes from, the execution of a trade is still exclusively up to you. Against this background, you should therefore be encouraged to implement your own trading ideas and at the same time act with full responsibility.

You have to learn to deal with losing and accept that losing is simply an integral part of successful trading. At the beginning of the book we spoke of costs in this context. Of course, you want to keep the costs low, but you cannot avoid them. And with this understanding, you must also face the losses in trading.

If you realize in the analysis of your trading statistics, that your cumulative losses are higher than your cumulative profits, then of course action is required. Then it is necessary to analyze exactly which adjustments need to be made in order to turn the hit rate back in your favor.

The hit rate is therefore an important component in your money management strategy for analyzing and optimizing your results.

In summary, the hit rate gives us a good indication of how winning and losing is doing in the overall picture. But on its own, it is not meaningful.

In addition to the risk to be taken per trade, the risk/reward ratio, and the hit rate, we need a fourth element to really complete our consideration.

In the first chapter of the book, we looked at the different trading styles. We have come so far that we have aligned our risk exposure to the various trading styles accordingly. Our fourth element is at least partially related to trading styles. Because what distinguishes the different trading styles at first glance is the number of positions that can be opened and closed in an overall period. An intraday trader trades much more on a weekly or monthly basis than a swing or even a position trader. The intraday trader trades in the course of a week perhaps even more often than the position trader trades in one year.

Here, too, we can ask ourselves the question whether we can draw conclusions about the quality of the trader by looking at the number of trades. By now you know what this question is aiming at. Of course not. We need more information in order to correctly evaluate the number of trades executed—the trading frequency.

If we hear, for example, from a position trader that he has traded 300 trades in a year, then this statement may make us ponder. If we hear the same statement from an intraday trader, then this figure seems completely natural to us; perhaps we would have expected even more.

However, we can gain even more information by looking at the trading frequency. If a trader executes 300 trades per year, the question arises to what extent his risk management is geared towards this. What does his individual position risk look like and what is his overall risk?

Many traders do not think about these connections at the beginning of their careers. Since access to the financial markets is now as easy as ordering a book, newcomers run the risk of rashly and too quickly rushing into the markets. With a few clicks an account is capitalized, the first positions are opened and a few happy trades later the trading world is fine. Loss control? Wrong! Profit target? Well. Position size? It's a bit different. You can imagine where this is going. And that's why it was important that you thought about risk management and that's why it was essential that you learn the individual elements of professional money management.

Let us now bring these four elements together and no longer look at them in isolation, but in interaction with each other.

Trust your statistics . . . The significance of risk, risk/reward ratio, hit rate, and trading frequency in practice

With our four elements presented, we can professionalize our money management and evaluate our trading results in context.

Let's start with the risk. Risk limitation is an essential part of our considerations and is the only way to ensure your long-term trading success. But if we limit the consideration to the risk, we will not get far. The mere statement that you use 1% of your trading account per trade as risk shows that you limit your risk, but nothing more.

It's good if you can also put the risk you have taken in relation to the profit you can make. Especially if the profit is higher than the risk you have to accept. However, what matters here is not what is possible, but what was actually possible—what was achieved. Looking at the risk/reward ratio will only give you the right clues for your risk and money management as well as the optimization of your trading results if you look at the realized risk/reward ratio. However, just looking at the realized risk/reward ratio alone will not help you optimize your trading results.

Then let us take the hit rate into consideration. To achieve a high hit rate is the wish of most traders. However, it is also not usable in isolation. If, on the other hand, you look at the hit rate in relation to the risk/reward ratio achieved, you will get the relevant information you need to optimize your overall results. There you go—that's one step further.

Finally, the trading frequency was the subject of our considerations. Intraday traders trade a lot, position traders rather less. According to this rule of thumb, we could also quickly wipe this topic aside. We could, but we don´t. Due to the fact that there is also important and essential information hidden for us, which is particularly important in combination with the hit rate or the realized risk/reward ratio.

With these elements, our considerations are complete and finally there is movement in our analysis. Let's just bring these elements together:

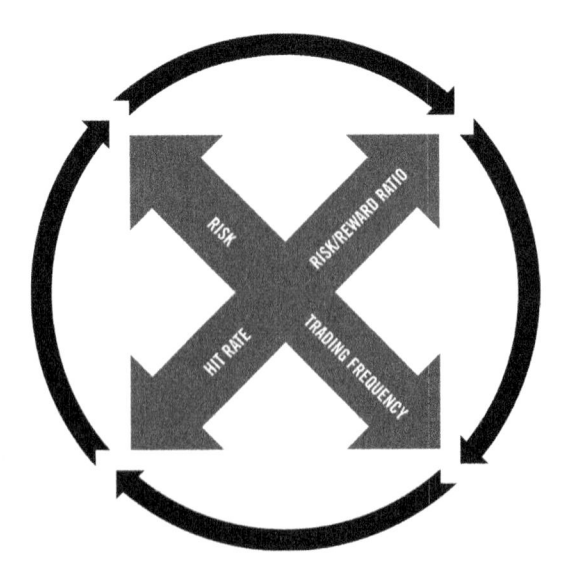

Figure 31: The "Money Management Matrix" shows the interaction of the four elements of professional risk and money management.

We can use the "Money Management Matrix" to look at the interaction of position or overall risk, the realized risk/reward ratio, the hit rate, and the trading frequency. The "Money Management Matrix" is a perfect tool to analyze and consider your own trading results. The matrix also supports you in planning and determining your future trading strategy.

At the beginning of this section, the use of a trading journal was suggested. For good reason. Only if you document your trading activities can you evaluate them statistically. It is not about calculating complex formulas and values. On the contrary, in the vast majority of cases, the bottom line is to look at the summed-up elements in their entirety and compare them. And the hit rate can only be calculated from the total sum of all trades.

Let's assume that you have set up such a trading journal and determined concrete values for your hit rate, your trading frequency, and your realized risk/reward ratio. You already know the risk you are taking before opening a position, independent of a trading journal.

For example,[11] you started with your trading account of $10,000 and you analyze your results at the end of the year.[12] You will find out that you have executed a total of 100 trades. With every single trade you have taken over a risk of 1% of your trading account, i.e., an absolute amount of $100.[13] Overall, you were able to achieve a realized risk/reward ratio of 1.5 with a hit rate of 50%. How can we judge this result?

Let these figures have some effect on you at first. What do you think? What results are likely to be possible if, for example, you have realized these figures at the end of a year? After all, you "only" take a risk of $100 per trade.

---

[11] In our following considerations we deliberately leave out the costs and fees of the trades, the systematics are important to us. Let's keep it "simplified"!

[12] Of course, you can also transfer the described information to shorter periods of time.

[13] For the sake of simplicity we keep this amount constant as well. In practice, it naturally makes sense to adjust the absolute amount gradually to the current account size.

Risk and Money Management for Day and Swing Trading

Trading account	$10,000
Risk in percent	1.0%
Hit rate	50%
Risk/reward ratio	1.5
Risk in US Dollar	$100
Trading frequency	100
Total profit	$2,500

Figure 32: The elements of the "Money Management Matrix" in action.

We can state that you have closed with a total profit of 25% of your trading account! Specifically, your realized risk/reward ratio of 1.5 not only enabled you to offset each individual loss, but also to record an additional profit per winning trade. Although you ended every second trade in the red, you were able to trade more than profitably. You owe this to your realized risk/reward ratio of 1.5!

What would your result look like if you had only achieved a realized risk/reward ratio of 1? We can calculate this quickly in our heads. The result is zero.

In conclusion, we can state that profitable trading is guaranteed up to a realized risk/reward ratio of slightly above 1 and a hit rate of 50%. The extent to which the result then achieved will help you in the development of your trading account is, of course, another matter.

Let's look at another example: Let's say you have a hit rate of only 40% with otherwise the same parameters. What is your total profit now? Or are you already in the red zone?

In fact, neither. With a realized risk/reward ratio of 1.5 and a hit rate of 40%, your trading results are exactly zero! They are neither in profit nor in loss—after all is finished.

Trading account	$10,000
Risk in percent	1.0%
Hit rate	40%
Risk/reward ratio	1.5
Risk in US Dollar	$100
Trading frequency	100
Total profit	$0

Figure 33: The elements of the "Money Management Matrix" in action I. We have lowered the hit rate to 40%.

In other words, in conclusion, you need significantly less than half the number of winners to trade profitably. However, you must then pay strict attention to your realized risk/reward ratio. If you fall below a risk/reward ratio of 1.5 with a realized hit rate of 40%, you will incur an overall loss.

In this context, we can look at another point that we need to assess our trading strategy. We have concluded that the hit rate, trading frequency, and risk/reward ratio are closely related. The hit rate is also a good starting point for determining whether a strategy can be profitable in itself. In order to determine this, we need to take another closer look at the hit rate and trading frequency.

To stay with our first example, we can deduce the extent to which our strategy is profitable at all from the fact that we have made a profit of $150 per trade in one half of our 100 trades and a loss of $100 per trade in the other half. We can calculate the "expected value" from this.

To do this, we have to multiply the hit rate by the average winners and subtract the loser rate multiplied by the average losers. What sounds complicated is easy to calculate in practice.

(Hit rate * Average of all winning trades)
- (Loser rate * Average of all losing trades) = Expected value

How do you get the average of all winners or losers? You simply add up all the profits made and divide them by the number of trades that are closed in profit. You proceed in the same way for the average of the losers.

Applied to our first example we can calculate the expected value:

(50% * $150) - ((1-50%) * $100) = Expected value
$75 - $50 = Expected value = $25

What does this mean for our trading strategy? In the end, this means nothing else than that we achieve a profit of $25 on average with each trade. No matter whether the individual trade is a winner or a loser, on average we achieve a profit of $25 under the given circumstances. This is a reassuring fact and once again clearly shows that it is not the individual trade that counts, but the totality of all trades. And of course, this also means that we can and must optimize exactly this whole!

We can also calculate the expected value for our second example, in which we assumed a hit rate of 40%.

(40% * $150)-((1-40%) * $100 = Expected value
$60 - $60 = Expected value = $0

This confirms our previous calculation. The result here is also zero. If you are trading like in the second example, you do not move any further. A trade won't get you anywhere, any more than it will throw you back. However, in the end you are always on the borderline of an overall loss.

So, if you want to use the expected value as an assessment criterion for your personal trading strategy, then make sure that it is positive. As soon as the expected value falls into the negative range, you lose money on average with every single trade!

This is an important recommendation for your upcoming trades. Be consistent in the selection of your positions and only enter into trades where the probability appears high that you can actually achieve your planned risk/reward ratio. In this sense: quality before quantity!

There is one more point we need to address before we can continue our reflections. So far, our considerations have always been based on the assumption that you either realize the loss in full or the profit in the planned amount. There is nothing in between. You can easily imagine that in practice you will also realize trades that will be somewhere in between in their results. This in turn is a question of trade management, which we will deal with in the next chapter, among others. Until then, we'll stick with the "either/or" approach.

With the help of the "Money Management Matrix," the mutual dependence and influence of the four different elements can also be depicted and recognized very well. In fact, these are both directly and indirectly related and influence each other. If we change a single element of our matrix, we change the overall result. You can take advantage of this fact for your planning of the overall result.

What does this mutual influence look like? Let's look at your trading frequency, for example. Suppose you plan to double your trading frequency from—say—100 trades to 200 trades. This way you double your trading result under otherwise identical circumstances.

Trading account	$10,000
Risk in percent	1.0%
Hit rate	50%
Risk/reward ratio	1.5
Risk in US Dollar	$100
Trading frequency	200
Total profit	$5,000

Figure 34: The elements of the "Money Management Matrix" in action II. We've doubled the trading frequency.

Risk and Money Management for Day and Swing Trading

What effects does this have on your risk, for example? In the same step, of course, you also double your overall risk. If you do not include this in your considerations, you can very quickly fall behind.

Let's consider another point: Assuming you increase your planned risk/reward ratio from 1.5 to 3 with immediate effect, what does this mean for your overall result? This will certainly increase. What do you think—under otherwise identical circumstances—by how much will your overall result probably change?

Trading account	$10,000
Risk in percent	1.0%
Hit rate	50%
Risk/reward ratio	3.0
Risk in US Dollar	$100
Trading frequency	100
Total profit	$10,000

Figure 35: The elements of the "Money Management Matrix" in action III. We have doubled the risk/reward ratio from 1.5 to 3 in our planning.

Your overall result has not only doubled, no, it has quadrupled! But before you rush into enthusiasm, let us be realistic. How will the change in the planned risk/reward ratio affect your hit rate? We can say in advance that a change in the risk/reward ratio will also result in a change in the hit rate. Whether you will then also achieve a hit rate of 50% is questionable. As already described, you do not need this to be profitable. However, your overall result in this interaction will most likely be below the quadrupling achieved above.

After all, what happens if you change your hit rate? Assuming you can increase your hit rate from 50% to 60%. Out of 100 trades, 60 trades end in a profit. This alone will of course increase your overall result.

Trading account	$10,000
Risk in percent	1.0%
Hit rate	60%
Risk/reward ratio	1.5
Risk in US Dollar	$100
Trading frequency	100
Total profit	$5,000

Figure 36: The elements of the "Money Management Matrix" in action IV. We have increased the hit rate from 50% to 60%.

If the other elements remain the same, improving your hit rate from 50% to 60% allows you to double your overall result. This means that with 10 more winning trades you can double your profit! Unfortunately, this is not linear. If you should then increase your hit rate from 60% to 70%, your result based on our example calculation will be $7,500.

A positive development in our "Money Management Matrix" allows us to increase the other elements as well. Imagine that you increase your trading frequency with this improved hit rate! You can further improve your results by not only improving one component but by improving the other components as well. We will take a closer look at this at the end of this chapter.

In conclusion, we can now state that with the "Money Management Matrix," you have a powerful instrument in your hands with which you can raise your trading results to a new level by making targeted changes to the individual components!

Do good things better: How to optimize your money management and improve your trading results!

We have seen from several examples that you can control your money management precisely with the four elements of the matrix. We would now like to take the opportunity to further deepen our planning and considerations with the aim of improving your trading results with the given means.

In doing so, we take another close look. Which element do we have to change and how in order to achieve better results under otherwise equal circumstances? Where can we compensate for weaknesses by deepening strong elements?

The discussion of these questions is important for you, because when analyzing your trading history, you not only will come across points where you already have strengths, but also discover points where you can still improve.

Let's start with the strengths. Where can we build on existing strengths and use them in turn to improve the overall result?

Imagine that you realize a hit rate of 60%. Six out of ten trades are closed with a profit. If we stick to our already known parameters, this means that you will have made a profit of 50% of your original trading account!

Actually, you could be quite happy with that, couldn't you? Nevertheless, let us take this value as the basis of our optimization strategy in order to increase the overall result even further.

To enable you to perform the calculations based on your own results, we will take a quick look at the formula behind our calculations:

(TF * HR * RRR * R) - (TF * (1 - HR) * R) = Overall trading result

Where TF is the trading frequency, HR the hit rate, RRR the risk/reward ratio and R the risk.

What value can we now adjust to increase the results under otherwise identical circumstances?

First and foremost, the trading frequency is the most appropriate. If you imagine that you simply have to execute more trades—for example, 200 instead of 100 trades—to increase the total profit, then it sounds logical at first. However, you will need to find twice as many entry opportunities with the same quality as your previous trades. To what extent this is actually feasible is questionable. Nevertheless, this is an opportunity for you.

Trading account	$10,000
Risk in percent	1.0%
Hit rate	60%
Risk/reward ratio	1.5
Risk in US Dollar	$100
Trading frequency	100
Total profit	$5,000

Trading account	$10,000
Risk in percent	2.0%
Hit rate	60%
Risk/reward ratio	1.5
Risk in US Dollar	$200
Trading frequency	100
Total profit	$10,000

Figure 37 and 38: The hit rate of 60% already generates a total profit of 50%. By increasing the risk to 2%, the result also can be doubled.

Another possibility is to increase the individual risk per trade. Yes, you read that correctly! If you can show a clearly positive hit rate, you can increase your risk. Of course, not unlimited, but with a sense of proportion. So, you can certainly increase the risk from 1% to 1.5% or even 2%. This will increase your overall risk and you will have to draw up a new action plan in which you draw your line under the adjusted conditions. As a consequence, however, you implement the same number of trades, plan and realize an unchanged risk/reward ratio and increase your overall result by 50% or even 100%.

Of course, you need to keep a close eye on how your strategy is developing and you may need to change the parameters again if the results deviate significantly from your planning. However, under the conditions mentioned above, you can significantly improve your overall result in this way.

Of course, it is not easy to achieve a hit rate of 60%. Especially at the beginning of a trading career, it is difficult to achieve a hit rate that promises a positive overall result. Let us take as an example a hit rate of 30%, which in our case leads to a negative overall result. Our goal now is to achieve a positive overall result under these circumstances. There must be a "zero" in here at least! How can we achieve this?

The immediate first consequence of this is already clear. Down with the risk per trade!

In addition to reducing the risk, there is also a reduction in the risk/reward ratio!

The alert reader has already recognized it. Simply by adjusting the planned risk/reward ratio downwards, the overall result will be worse in purely mathematical terms under unchanged circumstances. This is true and remains true. But by lowering the risk/reward ratio and thus the profit target, we increase the probability that the trades entered into will turn into winners—which in turn increases the hit rate.

Trading account	$10,000
Risk in percent	1.0%
Hit rate	30%
Risk/reward ratio	1.5
Risk in US Dollar	$100
Trading frequency	100
Total profit	-$2,500

Trading account	$10,000
Risk in percent	0.5%
Hit rate	46%
Risk/reward ratio	1.2
Risk in US Dollar	$50
Trading frequency	100
Total profit	$60

Figure 39 and 40: Changes in the risk/reward ratio increase the probability of hits and thus increase the hit rate. At the same time the risk is reduced. As a result, the overall result improves.

In our example, we reduce the risk per trade by half to 0.5% of the trading account and lower the planned risk/reward ratio to 1.2. To get into the green zone, we need a hit rate of a little less than 46%. The lower risk/reward ratio means that this possibility exists, because the probability of winning increases.

In order to move from the red to the green area, these can be the possible measures that we can concretely take on the part of risk and money management. In addition, of course, it is also appropriate to investigate the reasons for the trading strategy, the methodology of the analysis, and your own personal approach to trading.

Let us consider another point. Let's assume that your analysis shows that your overall realized risk/reward ratio is 1.2. You want to improve your overall result. Which components can you strengthen for this?

At this point we can already state that under these conditions your hit rate must be above 45% to be profitable. It is likely to be above that because you will take your winnings faster and the goal to be achieved will be closer to your entry point.

For simplicity's sake, let's say you get another 50% hit rate, then you will generate a 10% profit on your trading account under the above circumstances. This is more than respectable and beats the results of many professional investors by far. To further increase your profit, you could of course increase your risk, although a moderate approach is preferable in this combination.

Trading account	$10,000
Risk in percent	1.0%
Hit rate	50%
Risk/reward ratio	1.2
Risk in US Dollar	$100
Trading frequency	100
Total profit	$1,000

Trading account	$10,000
Risk in percent	1.5%
Hit rate	50%
Risk/reward ratio	1.2
Risk in US Dollar	$150
Trading frequency	150
Total profit	$2,250

Figure 41 and 42: A low risk/reward ratio can be offset by increasing the trading frequency and a moderate increase in risk.

Another possibility is to increase the number of trades. Now we have already discussed this critical point above, but there is still a possibility of improving your results. In this case, a middle course can be a slight increase in risk to, for example, 1.5% and an increase in trading frequency. For example, an increase of 50 more trades executed. As a result, you have more than doubled your profits. Small measure, big effect.

We can stick to our view of risk and trading frequency and consider how we can optimize our overall result if we enter the market with only a small amount of risk. We don't need a table for this to be able to say as a rule of thumb that with a small risk to be taken per position we also have the possibility to trade more often and more aggressively. In other words, as long as our realized risk/reward ratio remains at least 1. If it falls below that, we will have to rethink our strategy in any case.

Let us go into the last example of our reflections. Imagine that you have developed a strategy that gives you a realized risk/reward ratio of 2.5 at the end of a trading year. Surely you can appreciate this result according to our previous examples. Your other parameters remain unchanged. What else can you change to improve the overall result?

Let's go over the "Money Management Matrix" together: Trade frequency? Yes, possibly. However, there are natural limits to your trading style. If you are a position trader, then you cannot execute several hundred trades at once per year. But an increase of perhaps 10% is possible. To do this, you may need to move into new markets or stocks that you are additionally incorporating into your analysis.

What about the hit rate? To what extent can this one still be turned around? Due to your high realized chance-risk ratio your hit rate will inevitably not exceed a certain range. Maybe you can still get a few percentage points out of it by means of a precise analysis, but large increases will most likely not be possible.

The hit rate and trading frequency will eventually find their natural limits. Especially the trading frequency cannot be increased infinitely, because from the point where you enter every trade that comes under your keys, this will have an immediate effect on your hit rate. Your hit rate will then drop again. Your trading frequency is ultimately determined by the specific opportunities on which your hit rate ultimately depends.

Trading account	$10,000
Risk in percent	1.0%
Hit rate	50%
Risk/reward ratio	2.5
Risk in US Dollar	$100
Trading frequency	100
Total profit	$7,500

Trading account	$10,000
Risk in percent	2.5%
Hit rate	55%
Risk/reward ratio	2.5
Risk in US Dollar	$250
Trading frequency	110
Total profit	$25,438

Figure 43 and 44: A high realized risk/reward ratio allows for a higher risk.

So that still leaves the risk. With a hit rate of 50%—as generally assumed—and a realized risk/reward ratio of 2.5, the way is clear for more aggressive action. In this case, you can increase your risk, because you will regularly receive a multiple of it back.

Ultimately, the increase in risk is also the only parameter that you can freely determine completely and independently. Always keep a sense of proportion here, because every rally has an end, but fortunately so does every bear market.

We can conclude our considerations of the "Money Management Matrix," but not without closing words. You have got to know the "Money Management Matrix" as a valuable tool that helps you to optimize your trading results. You got to know the individual components and set screws and we worked through several scenarios together to see how you could improve your results in different situations with the individual parameters. This is active money management at the highest level. This gives you the opportunity to tailor your trading to your own situation and use your trading capital effectively and profitably. The "Money Management Matrix" is not a scientific approach, but a source of inspiration for your own considerations. The idea of the matrix is to show you options to take your personal requirements into account when planning and implementing your trades. It is therefore essential that you carry out further analysis and develop your own ideas about how your personal "Money Management

Matrix" should be designed to work for you. You have already got to know the first approaches. The ball's in your court.

Finally, we want to go to the practice, where our three traders are already waiting to present their thoughts and results. In old tradition, Rick begins:

I didn't think I needed so much planning for my trading. On closer inspection, however, this makes perfect sense to me. I'm more of a spontaneous type. So, it is important that I have a plan that I can and must stick to. I have already done this in detail, but overall, there is still a need for action. Especially when I think about recording my trades regularly. As a day trader, there are already a few trades a week and a month. In total, I opened and closed almost 1,000 trades last year. I took the time to list my trades and create a precise statistic. Overall, I have already gained a lot of experience in trading. Here are my statistics:

Trading account	$5,000
Risk in percent	1.0%
Hit rate	44%
Risk/reward ratio	1.3
Risk in US Dollar	$50
Trading frequency	982
Total profit	$589

Figure 45: The trading statistics of Rick after one year and 982 executed trades.

I haven't really gotten that far yet. Although my instincts are wrong here, in percentage terms, I have made more than 11% profit. I might as well be proud of it. However, I have missed my overall goal by far. I had already suspected that I would not get that far with my amount at risk, but I had promised myself something more. However, when I look at the results, I can actually improve quite a bit. Position risk alone is therefore not the only factor.

I have noticed that my realized risk/reward ratio is below my planned one. I had set myself a realized risk/reward ratio of 1.5 and achieved only 1.3. Admittedly, I just got out too early—manually, on one or other trades—but I never thought that it would have such effects!

I still have to work on my hit rate. This is where I want to get close to 50%! Although I am already positive with my result of 44%, I simply have to hit more often with the low risk/reward ratio. One thing is for sure: I have to reconsider my planned result of $500 per month or increase the individual components of the "Money Management Matrix." Preferably both.

The good news is that I am now starting with an account that is more than 11%[14] larger, because the profit will stay on my trading account for now. In the future, I will also adjust my calculations for the position size every month so that I can correctly include the then-current account size. By doing so, I can put an extra lever here.

To achieve my goal, I have worked out the following plan. Accompanying this I will further deepen my knowledge in technical analysis.

Trading account	$5,589
Risk in percent	1.0%
Hit rate	48%
Risk/reward ratio	1.3
Risk in US Dollar	$56
Trading frequency	1,000
Total profit	$5,813

Figure 46: The new plan of Rick according to his achieved components of the "Money Management Matrix."

---

[14] We keep individual taxes out of our examples as they differ from country to country. Please be advised to do the calculation with your current taxes.

I imagine that I can adapt my expectations to the risk/reward ratio. I am simply impatient and especially in forex trading it can go back and forth quite a bit. That is why the 1.3 is now officially my target. I'm also sticking to the trading frequency of 1,000 trades, as that also worked quite well in the past. I have seven currency pairs under observation, which means that I can expect to make around 140 trades per currency pair a year. This can be achieved.

By correcting my planned risk/reward ratio downwards, I increase the probability that I will increase my hit rate. I imagine that in the first step this will bring me close to 48%. With my improved knowledge of technical analysis, I will also be able to produce better analysis. If I can implement this in such a way, then I will also achieve my planned goal. I'm really excited about that!

Rick had planned a very ambitious target of 120% profit. Now he has landed at just over 11%, which is already very respectable. Furthermore, it is also clear with Rick that the hit rate does not have to be 50% in order to trade profitably. His realized risk/reward ratio of 1.3 is also below his target value, but in combination with the hit rate he is in the green zone. It is important to note that with this combination he moves on a knife´s edge. If his hit rate falls below 44%, Rick runs the risk of sliding into an overall loss. Therefore, his approach to increase the hit rate in the future is the right measure. His idea of lowering the planned risk/reward ratio to 1.3 also makes sense to him. Especially if he acts aggressively and is rather impatient, he will hardly be able to achieve more. At the same time, he can increase the probability of his winners. We can already see in the calculation that Rick gets close to his goal in this way. In the positive case, he will even get above it, as he adjusts his position size calculations monthly to the current account size.

As a conclusion, we can state that even a small change in the hit rate, namely from 44% to 48%, has an immense effect on the overall results. For this reason, always pay attention to the quality of your positions to be opened! Furthermore, it is remarkable how even a small position with a small risk can achieve a big result over the trading frequency.

Before we go on to Anna, a word about the overall result of Rick. Although he has already performed excellently with 11% total profit, he is dissatisfied with the absolute result achieved. On the one hand this is understandable, because after all the work he would have expected more. On the other hand, a trading account like Rick's quickly reaches its limits. This is not to say that professional trading does not work under these circumstances. On the contrary, it does. This only means that the absolute results achieved must always be placed in relation to the starting point. Imagine if Rick had opened an account with $500,000 trading capital instead of an account with $5,000. With the same percentage profit of around 11%, the absolute result would be significantly different. For this reason, do not be misled by perceived small results. It is always the percentage results that count for the analysis. Always keep a sense of proportion here, too!

What are the experiences with Anna? What results can she show us?

Since the Apple trade already took me a couple of months and is still going, I naturally couldn't carry out as many trades as Rick. However, the other trades were already faster at the target or stop loss, so that also made a difference. I had set myself a total risk of $2,500 as limit. For me, this means not only being able to deal professionally with a series of losses, but also to execute several trades in parallel. Strictly speaking, I can put my total risk in the market at once by holding ten positions with one percent risk each. However, if all ten positions end in a loss at once, I am already done trading. I have therefore chosen a middle course and have set myself a maximum of five individual titles to hold in my portfolio at the same time. This gives me room for maneuvers in case all five end up in a loss. I always varied the risk to be taken per trade between 1% and 1.5%, as it suited. I also did not always reach my target risk/reward ratio of 2.5. This is mainly because I did not see the probability of achieving this in some positions. Instead, there were many trades where I thought it was very likely to reach 1.5 and 2.0. So, I am somewhere between 1.5 and 2.5 times the risk/reward ratio in single trading. All in all, this gives me a gratifying 1.8 in terms of the realized risk/reward ratio. My individual risk, as I said, was between 1% and 1.5% of my trading account. In total, I have an average individual risk of 1.24%. Overall, I can look back on 26 trades that I opened and closed last year. My hit rate was very good. I had 58% winners in the portfolio. My overall result is above my target figure, which confirms my actions.

Trading account	$25,000
Risk in percent	1.24%
Hit rate	58%
Risk/reward ratio	1.8
Risk in US Dollar	$310
Trading frequency	26
Total profit	$5,029

Trading account	$30,029
Risk in percent	1.30%
Hit rate	60%
Risk/reward ratio	2.0
Risk in US Dollar	$390
Trading frequency	30
Total profit	$9,369

Figure 47 and 48: Anna's result after 26 trades within one year and her optimization based on this.

I don't see any real need for optimization at the moment, so I'm looking at the "Money Management Matrix" for basic growth opportunities. I think I'll keep all parameters the same, but I'll see if I can make a few more trades and I'll also increase my average position risk a bit. For me, this means that I often take 1.5% of my trading account as position risk. In addition, I intend to raise my profit targets again somewhat, so that I arrive at a realized risk/reward ratio of 2.0 overall. I am ambitious in terms of the hit rate and will use all my skills to lead 60% of my trades to profit. These measures, together with my growing trading account, will bring me a lot further. By the way, I can adjust the calculation base after each trade, so that I can gain a few more percentage points.

Anna's approach was a spot-on landing. She entered the market with more risk where she saw opportunities and took a defensive stance where the opportunities were not so obvious. As a result, she has achieved her goal and generated a good 20% profit—this with a sense of proportion in individual and overall risk. Of course, the market has to play along, but if it doesn't, the hit rate quickly drops back to the middle range. Nevertheless, when it runs, it runs and Anna has adjusted exactly to it. The adjustment of her desired risk/reward ratio to market conditions has certainly also played its part in the success.

For you, this means again to keep a sense of proportion and to consider what you wish for and what is possible. This simply has to be emphasized again at this point!

As always, we ask Peter how he did with his trading and what results he achieved.

I had a mixed bag. I had already presented a trade to you and actually I had a whole series of winners afterwards, which strengthened my self-confidence. I thought I had reached my overall goal, but unfortunately a series of losses started from that moment on. This is also reflected in the hit rate of 39%. This is annoying, of course, but the bottom line is that I have made a profit after all. I had a lot of ups and downs in my account in that one year and I was in doubt more than once. If you keep making losses, it's just not fun anymore. But in the end, I finally got my act together. My realized risk/reward ratio of 1.67 helped me to survive this shaky period. Although I had firmly resolved not to disturb my trades, I could not hold back and closed many trades manually—either because I wanted to capture the win or avoid the loss. This also explains why I missed my target with a realized risk/reward ratio of 2.0. Nevertheless, I stuck with it, because with my manageable risk I have always been able to get excited about a new trade even after a series of losses. And I think that's what counts: Stick to it and keep going! In total I made eighty-seven trades and, in the end, I could look back on a profit of a little more than $400. From now on it can only go up!

Risk and Money Management for Day and Swing Trading

Trading account	$15,000
Risk in percent	0.75%
Hit rate	39%
Risk/reward ratio	1.67
Risk in US Dollar	$113
Trading frequency	87
Total profit	$404

Trading account	$15,404
Risk in percent	0.75%
Hit rate	45%
Risk/reward ratio	2.00
Risk in US Dollar	$116
Trading frequency	60
Total profit	$2,426

Figure 49 and 50: Peter's results after a year of ups and downs. Although he achieved a hit rate of only 39%, he was able to close the trading year on a positive note thanks to his realized risk/reward ratio of 1.67. For the optimization Peter has put special emphasis on the risk/reward ratio and the hit rate.

For the coming year, I have set up my "Money Management Matrix" in such a way that I will, of course, continue to take the risk I am prepared to take. That definitely helped me inside! I want to work hard on my hit ratio. Going from 39% to 45% is a really big increase, but I will be working even harder on the analysis methods and above all, I will pay more attention to the quality of my trades. This is then also reflected in the reduced trading frequency. I prefer to skip a trade I am not so convinced of and concentrate fully on the promising trades with a high probability of winning. This is *how I imagine achieving a risk/reward ratio of 2.0, as I had planned. Of course, this requires that I hold back during the trade and leave the trade alone. By doing so, I'll get to my goal after all!*

Peter has learned two of the most important rules in trading. No winning streak lasts forever and only those who continue can ultimately get further. For this very reason it is important to determine your position risk according to your own requirements. Rigid numbers won't help you there; it's up to you. Take the amount at which you are willing to continue during and after a losing streak. This is the only way to get out of the losing streak. Carry on . . . with a sense of proportion and strategy, but keep going. Stay on the ball, look for your opportunities and then open the new position as planned. Peter also touched on exactly the same point that we had already discussed. He has disrupted his trades and it is good that he now intends to stop doing exactly that. What is interesting about Peter's results is that despite a relatively low hit rate, he achieves a positive result, which in turn is due to his realized risk/reward ratio. So, when he says that this is exactly what he wants to increase in the future, then that is the right impulse. Peter solves the dilemma between a high hit rate and a higher risk/reward ratio by trying to improve the quality of his trades. He wants to act less accordingly. It remains to be seen, of course, whether this will succeed. Nevertheless, it is always a good idea to be selective and critical in the choice of positions.

A brief summary of the most important facts:

> Hit rate and trading frequency are important elements of professional money management and complete the consideration of risk management.

> Hit rate and trading frequency alone are not relevant. Only in combination with other elements they can be analyzed meaningfully.

> Risk, risk/reward ratio, hit rate, and trading frequency can be combined to form the "Money Management Matrix." The "Money Management Matrix" indicates that the four elements are directly and indirectly dependent on each other. Weaknesses in one variable can be compensated by strengths in

the other. The higher the realized risk/reward ratio, the lower the hit rate will be and vice versa. A high trading frequency can compensate for a low realized risk/reward ratio. With a high hit rate, the risk can be increased as long as the realized risk/reward ratio is greater than 1. A realized risk/reward ratio of 1.5 is a good starting point and ensures the overall profit, even if the hit rate is below 50%.

CHAPTER 6:
Risk and Money Management 2.0

Up to this point, we have dealt intensively with all relevant aspects of risk and money management. You are now a professional in risk and money management and are far ahead of the masses in the market. Nevertheless, there is still some room for improvement. Although the points shown so far are perfectly sufficient to make trading profitable in the long term, this does not mean that we could not do even better.

At this point, we would like to expand the money management to include "trade management" and discuss various ways in which you can improve your results while keeping the risk per position unchanged.

We will deal with the topic of stop loss, the variation of entries and exits and a step-by-step entry and exit from positions. In addition to optimizing the "Money Management Matrix," these strategies should help us to achieve the best possible results with our trades.

But also, investors who do not want to sell their positions, but at the same time do not want to accept disproportionate risk in the event of a loss, will find an interesting method of loss limitation in this chapter.

Limitation or let run? What effects does a trailing stop have on your risk and money management?

In the course of the discussion on loss limitation in risk management, we have already dealt with the stop loss. With the stop loss we marked the point at which the probability of our strategy no longer works. At this point, it no longer makes sense to stay in the position and speculate on a positive outcome—the stop loss automatically limits our losses by being realized directly.

We had always assumed in our considerations that the stop loss is placed in the market and remains there unchanged until it is either triggered or dissolved because the trade reached the profit target. "Either-or" was the premise. We're going to change that now. Whereas we have so far looked at the stop loss exclusively from a risk management perspective, we are now expanding our view to professional trade management. An important part of professional trade management is to make a decision whether and to what extent the stop loss is moved during a trade.

By this stage, we should already have clarity about the sense and purpose of a trailed stop loss. Of course, we move the stop loss exclusively in order to secure accumulated profits. We do not move the stop loss in order to increase possible losses. There can, therefore, only be one direction in which the stop loss is moved or tightened: towards profit. In this way, the initial stop loss becomes the trailing stop.

You can easily imagine that there are countless approaches to use a trailing stop. The approaches are as numerous as there are traders in the markets.

Now we want to deal with the trailing stop in general. To what extent does it even make sense to trail the stop loss? Already, at this point, the opinions among the traders differ. While some of them start trailing after the first points, others leave the stop loss unchanged until they are close to the target. Others do none of this. They leave their stop loss unchanged until the trade closes either in profit or loss. If you question all three about who is doing it the right way, each one will claim to be correct.

This alone shows you that the trailing stop is not so much a purely mathematical topic, but rather an emotional one. This is also about dealing with losses and responsibility for one's own decisions. This is often shown by the fact that traders shift the trailing stop so close to the current price that they are already thrown out of the trade the very next moment. In hindsight it is then easy to say: "I wanted to let the trade go, but the price went into my trailing stop and so I had to close the position." In this way, the decision on how to proceed is conveniently outsourced to the market. As a consequence, this means that traders are shirking their own responsibility for the trade and at the same time avoiding consistent decisions. It is obvious that this is not part of professional trading and concrete success planning. Accordingly, it is already recommended at this point to use a trailing stop with a sense of proportion. Profit protection and loss limitation: Yes! Outsourcing of decisions: No.

With this in mind, let's look at two specific techniques for using the trailing stop.

The first method is again all about chart analysis. Just as we use the technical analysis to define our stop loss for loss limitation when planning a trade, we also look for corresponding points in the chart for the trailing stop that meet the same criteria. Here, too, we have to ask ourselves the question at which point in the chart the probability is no longer given that the trade will close with a profit.

These points are regularly the corresponding low points of an up move and the corresponding high points of a downward movement.

Let us illustrate this with a chart picture:

Figure 51: EUR/USD, 4-hour chart (one candle = 4 hours). After a steep rally, the pair builds a top and a strong resistance and forms a trading range between $1.11798 and $1.10701. After the last rebound of the resistance a short-trade is opened to profit from a falling Euro. After opening the position, the price falls dynamically to the support of the range and further on to the next support $1.09936. The stop loss is trailed during the course of the trade from one lower high to the other. The trade is partially closed when the targets 1 and 2 are reached. The last third is closed when the trailing stop at point 6 is reached. Source: www.tradingview.com

We see EUR/USD in the 4-hour chart. After a rally up to $1.11830, the pair built a resistance in that area, which was tested several times. With the first correction of the former rally, a support was built which was then tested two times. After the currency pair didn´t manage to break the resistance but built a little triple-top instead, it was obvious that the uptrend had come to an end. The entry point into a short trade is the breakout under the low of the triple-top. Once the price breaks this little support, the position should be opened. The entry price at this point is $1.11287. We put the initial stop loss to limit losses above the resistance $1.11810. As you see, we add a few extra pips for our safety. Our initial risk at position opening is 51 pips. We can find our first profit target at the low of the range at $1.10701. From entry to our target we have a potential of 58 pips, which gives a planned risk/reward ratio of 1.13. Not so much, but maybe we can go for more. A glance at the chart also reveals that we have the chance for two more profit targets, as there is a support at $1.09936. At this point, we can exit another part of our position with a profit of 135 pips and therefore a risk/reward ratio of 2.64. The third profit target is at the next support level at $1.09437. If the price drops down to this point, we will exit the third part of our position and close the trade for good. Please note that the possibility to reach the first profit target is significantly higher than reaching the second and even the third one.

After opening the trade, the price of the currency pair moves dynamically downwards and we are immediately at the first profit target exiting our first third of the position. As expected, the price bounces there and forms a lower high at point 1. We want to take the opportunity to adjust our stop loss to this level. But where exactly?

The first impulse is sure to follow the stop loss directly above the high of the price in the chart. And this is exactly the reason why the trailing stop is often accompanied by unsatisfactory results. If we place the stop loss too close to the price, we increase the probability that the stop loss will be triggered when the market tests the previous level again.

Therefore, always give some room between your stop loss and the last absolute high or low. Even at the risk of taking a smaller position, this procedure will save you from many losing trades. Simply because the market still has room to move and breathe.

We are therefore not placing our trailing stop directly above the marked high at $1.10929, but 5 pips above it at $1.10979. Especially in the 4-hour chart, 5 pips are hardly noticeable. In the smaller timeframes, of course, things look different. There 5 pips can already make up the entire profit of a trade. Accordingly, the distance there should be smaller—2 pips may be sufficient. If you want to make sure you are not unhappily stopped out, then add some more pips.

With the trailing stop our overall situation has changed. We now no longer have a loss limitation stop, but a profit protection stop! Our new stop loss is already 30 pips lower than our entry price. A very comfortable situation!

The second profit target is reached through a series of higher highs and lows. For us, this is another good opportunity to tighten the stop loss again and again. Not to $1.10203 at point 6, but to $1.10253. After all, we want to secure profits! This means that—no matter what—we are already 103 pips in profit with 2/3 of our position.

Ultimately, our patience is rewarded as our second profit target is reached at $1.09936; the second third of the position is closed with a profit of 135 pips and a risk/reward ratio of 2.64. With the speculation of a further decline of the price the last third stays in the trade. But as every move comes to an end, the price recovers on the support and begins a new uptrend exiting the last third of our trade at point 6 with a profit of 103 pips.

Summing it up, with this trade, we made 98 pips with a risk/reward ratio of 1.9.

Maybe you ask yourself why we used three profit targets instead of just one. The answer is easy. It is all about taking the chances and getting the most out of a trade. We will come back to this later.

A conclusion we can draw is that a trade always needs air to breathe. Therefore, do not pull the trailing stop too close to the price; otherwise, there is a high risk that you will be stopped out. And you don't really want to be thrown out of the market. In fact, you want to reach your profit target, right? The stop loss is intended to protect you against disproportionate losses on the way there in the first step and to preserve your accumulated profits in the second step. Don't let the stop loss throw you out of the market! Keep this in mind when you place and trail your stop loss.

Another way to trail the stop loss is to use a fixed percentage or a fixed number of points. In many trading platforms, this can already be set automatically. Your stop loss will then be automatically moved further and further until the trade either runs into the profit target or is terminated by the stop loss. Of course, this sounds very comfortable at first. A trade that manages itself. This is almost too good to be true . . .

It is obvious that this approach is often suboptimal. The explanation is simple. Let's assume that we have trailed our stop loss in our long-term EUR/USD trade every 25 pips. What would have happened?

Let's take a look at the chart picture as well:

Figure 52: EUR/USD, 4-hour chart (one candle = 4 hours). The stop loss is trailed 25 pips above the current price. Source: www.tradingview.com

We have the identical chart from above. The only thing we change is the trailing stop. Assuming that we trail the stop every 25 pips, we move the stop loss in a way that we always have a distance of 25 pips from the current price to the stop loss. Soon after we have opened the trade, the stop is moved, lowering the risk of the position and securing first profits.

Since we have a high momentum after our entry, the first 25 pips profit is quickly reached. No matter what—this is what we have already earned!

As the price continues to drop in the direction of our first target, we keep on securing our profits. With the arrival at the first target we exit one third of the trade with a 58 pips profit and a secured profit of 33 pips due to our trailing stop. As price falls further after we exited our first third, it reached a low at $1.10620. With a distance of 25 pips our trailing stop is now at $1.10870, giving us a secured profit of 41 pips for our remaining two thirds of the position!

Since every move comes to an end at some point, the dynamic downward movement that has brought our trade so quickly into profit and to our first target also ends with a pullback. The price begins to rise and from the low at $1.10620, the price goes over our trailing stop at $1.10870 and we close our trade with a realized gain of 41 pips for our last two thirds.

In total we have made a profit of 46 pips with this trade. In comparison to the risk we have taken for this trade, we have realized a risk/reward ratio of 0.9.

How should we judge this? Profit is profit and therefore good. Especially since it was also generated in a relatively short period of time. That is also correct. Nevertheless, we had another target in mind. We wanted to achieve not only 46 pips, but at least 98 pips. That's twice as much! However, we must also admit, in fairness, that these 98 pips were gained in a much longer period of time, as we have already seen.

You have certainly already realized that at this point there can be no 100% recommendation for action. If you are on the hunt for quick wins in a very dynamic and impulsive environment, then you are well advised to use the second method. The other side of the coin is that you are regularly stopped out in intermediate corrections and the move then continues without you. This is exactly where the two variants differ.

As a result, we can state that a tight stop loss—for whatever reason—practically forces a quick exit from the position. You will then take profits more regularly, but they will always be lower than if you continue to place your stops in a more deliberate way. Ultimately, it is also the state of the market that determines whether a trailing stop is successful and meaningful. In a strong trend, the danger of being unhappily stopped out is less than in a sideways movement. Accordingly, a further profit-securing stop in a sideways movement makes more sense and a tight stop loss in a strong trend.

Perhaps the "Money Management Matrix" inevitably comes to mind during our discussion. In fact, a trailing stop has concrete effects on our success planning according to the "Money Management Matrix." What are they?

By trailing the stop loss, we leave the either/or decision and intervene in the current trade. Although we plan a concrete risk/reward ratio in advance of a trade, we reduce the chances of achieving it by adjusting the stop loss. A pullback could throw us easily out of the trade.

There are consequences. If we proceed in this way on a regular basis, in retrospect our realized risk/reward ratio will be reduced. For example, we go from 1.5 to 1.3, which alone does not necessarily mean anything, but we must be aware of this fact.

The realized risk/reward ratio is falling because we take our profits earlier. This also has a consequence. Our profits will be smaller, but still there. The hit rate will therefore increase—from 50% to 55% for example.

If we close the positions faster because we are simply stopped out earlier, then we have the opportunity to enter more trades. This is solely because the previously tied capital is now available for new trades again. This in turn has an impact on our trading frequency. It will increase provided that the opportunities are adequate. Maybe from 100 trades a year to 120 trades.

That leaves the risk. What does it mean for the risk we take if the hit rate is increased, the trading frequency increases and the risk/reward ratio is reduced? First of all, we have already established that a high hit rate also justifies a higher risk. In principle, we can implement this here as well. Maybe from 1.0% to 1.25%. By pulling the stop loss behind the price, we automatically and gradually reduce the risk and can therefore justify a higher stake. On the other hand, the number of trades will naturally increase the overall risk. We must give this point the appropriate importance and keep our results under constant review.

Let's take a look at a possible scenario according to a trailing stop:

Trading account	$10,000
Risk in percent	1.0%
Hit rate	50%
Risk/reward ratio	1.5
Risk in US Dollar	$100
Trading frequency	100
Total profit	$2,500

Trading account	$10,000
Risk in percent	1.25%
Hit rate	55%
Risk/reward ratio	1.3
Risk in US Dollar	$125
Trading frequency	120
Total profit	$3,975

Figure 53 and 54: Comparison of the results in the "Money Management Matrix" without trailing stop and with trailing stop. By managing the position in a targeted manner, the overall trading results can be improved.

We see that even slight changes to the individual components of the "Money Management Matrix" can lead to a significant improvement in profits. The decisive factor here is the realized risk/reward ratio. The closer it gets to the 1, the higher the hit rate must be. Accordingly, it is important to leave both elements in a healthy relationship. Profit taking yes, but not at any price!

With this, we can also end the discussion of the trailing stop and conclude that a trailing stop is an adequate means to manage a trade professionally. The prerequisite for this is that the loss limitation and profit protection stop does not become a "trade termination stop." Which of the presented variants you choose is a question of personal style and taste. It is also perfectly okay if you do not interfere with your trades at all.

Let us look at our three traders at the end of the topic. How do they deal with the issue of trailing stops? Rick, how do you feel about a trailing stop?

I've always been annoyed when I first ran into the profit, only to watch it disappear again and I'm stopped out in the loss as a result. The trailing stop is therefore a good opportunity for me to at least partially protect my profits. For me, the default method actually makes sense. In the future, I will always trail the stop loss ten pips behind the current price. When I then approach the target area, I will place the stop loss more aggressively on the price. I'm thinking about five pips. This way I make sure I don't have to give back so much of my accumulated profits.

Rick's assessment is comprehensible. The closer he gets to the profit, the more annoyed he is that he has to give the profits back. This is understandable, and it also fits in with his aggressive self-assessment to bring the stop loss in the target area very close to the price. On the one hand, he won't have to give away many pips of his winnings this way, but, on the other hand, Rick often won't reach his profit target. This has a corresponding impact on his realized risk/reward ratio; especially since Rick already keeps his planned risk/reward ratio relatively low, he quickly runs the risk of worsening his overall results significantly.

How does Anna plan the management of her position trades?

With my time horizon, a trailing stop definitely makes sense. Especially when I consider the political and economic influences to which a company and its shares are exposed over the months, I have to secure my accumulated profits. However, for me the trailing stop is still a stop that better is not to be triggered. After all, I want to be rewarded for my patience. Especially as I do not execute that many trades per year, I cannot afford to disturb my positions. I will proceed accordingly after the technical analysis to identify suitable points where I can place the trailing stop. But like I said, for me, this is just a worst-case scenario.

Anna sticks to her strategy. Insurance, yes, but just in case. Otherwise, she lets the trade run unhindered.

Where does Peter see approaches for a trailing stop in trading with futures?

With me, it's one thing to lose. Especially because last year did not go so well and I have planned an ambitious risk/reward ratio for my next trades. But when I think about my hit rate, there is certainly room for improvement. With a trailing stop, I can have a direct influence on the hit rate. However, I don't think that I can then still realize a risk/reward ratio of 2.0. That would mean that the price would go even further than I had planned anyway. Then why don't I set an even higher target?! All in all, I think I'll leave my stop loss unchanged. The only thing I can think of is to move the stop loss to my entry after the price has moved into the range of my simple risk. Then I leave my risk practically the same, only with the difference that I can no longer run into a loss.

Peter's considerations reveal another interesting point. Assuming that the risk remains unchanged, it makes sense to move the stop loss to the entry price at the moment when a risk/reward ratio of 1 is reached. The risk remains unchanged, except that the accumulated profit and no longer the own capital is at risk. On the other hand, the probability of a stop loss increases accordingly, as the stop loss is again adjusted to the current price.

Ultimately, it is always a matter of weighing whether and where the stop loss will lag behind the price.

Now that we have discussed the trailing stop in detail, we can use the knowledge gained to refine this area even further. Perhaps there is still room for improvement in a step-by-step entry and exit into and from a trade.

Get in, get out, move up: This is how you can increase your winnings with no change in risk!

Our trading results can already be significantly influenced by using a trailing stop. Especially with regard to the "Money Management Matrix," this can result in interesting opportunities for us. We can now go even further and analyze the impact of a gradual entry and exit of a position on our trading results. First of all, however, you should know that at this point we are dealing with techniques and strategies for advanced traders. Advanced in two senses. On the one hand, these strategies are already somewhat more complex and require more intensive calculations than the previous ideas. On the other hand, these strategies can only be fully implemented once your trading account has reached a certain size.

Let's start by getting into a trade right away. Up to now, we have always taken the full extent of our consideration into account. This is over now! We now want to take a closer look at two options for a step-by-step entry into the market.

A variant of a step-by-step entry—a "Scaling In"—into the market consists of placing a portion of the planned position in the market ahead of the actual entry signal. With this aggressive variant you are already in the market when the desired movement actually starts. Only when you reach your entry signal you increase the position to the full amount.

If, on the other hand, your strategy does not work out, you only take a reduced risk with your sub-position, with which you are stopped out in the event of a loss. The advantage of this method is that you can benefit from movement from the very beginning without disproportionately increasing your risk.

The second way to get started in several steps is to follow a trend over time. The strategy here is to gradually increase the position after it is already in profit. In this way you can secure the chance of disproportionate profits without taking any additional risk. With this approach, active risk and trade management is essential!

Let's take a look at the first possibility by gradually entering a trade:

Figure 55: NASDAQ 100 INDEX, weekly chart (one candle = one week). After a steep rally the Nasdaq100 Index fell to point 1, rose from there to point 2 and then fell back to point 3, forming a higher low within a trend correction. With the breakout through point 2 a continuation of the uptrend is likely. A previous entry provides additional chances of winning. Source: www.tradingview.com

We see the Nasdaq 100 Index in the weekly chart. As a result of the sharp correction of the former up move, the Nasdaq 100 has fallen to point 1 at 3,787 points. From there, a first move up again into the trend led to point 2 which was forming a slighter new high at 4,739 points. The following down move could not mark a new low, but came to a halt at point 3 at 3,888 points. With these three points and the classic approach to enter the market with the break of point 2 we can open a trade with the idea of following the trend once point 2 is reached and broken. So as assumed from point 3, the Nasdaq 100 resumed its initial upward momentum with a series of green candles. But this move didn´t lead to a new high, instead the price stopped in the last third of the range and went sideways for a while offering a good chance to enter the market at a better price.

We can increase our chances of winning by not entering the market at once, but by splitting the position into several sub-positions. We leave the planned entry point and the initial stop loss unchanged. We are also leaving the size of the position unchanged overall. These are the basic conditions for our first variant.

At this point let us assume that we divide our position into two partial positions. As usual, we want to give a part of it to the market when the point of entry is reached. With the other part we want to enter the market earlier. The stop loss is identical in each case, so that trade management of the overall position can be done in the usual way when the entry point is reached.

To open our first partial position, we need to identify a point in the chart where there is a probability that the price will move in the direction we want.

This point is the breakout of the little range and its high at 4,574 points. When this high is taken out, chances are high that the price correction is over after all and the former uptrend is to be continued including the break of point 2, where we want to complete our trade with the second half of the position.

Let´s take a closer look. Within the little range the Nasdaq 100 forms a higher low again which is followed by a long green candle embracing the red one. We can see this by the fact that after a short correction the price is already rising again and continues the up move. This fact confirms our positive assessment.

A continuation of the up move and a breaking of the high at point 2 thus seems very likely. This in turn gives us the right to open our sub-position at the entry 1. If the market now continues its up move, we will already be in profit with 165 points when the second part of our position is opened at our entry 2 at 4,739 points. From this moment on the position is complete and the management goes as usual.

As a result of the first partial position we already have a profit of 165 points compared to a complete entry! And the best part is that our absolute risk is unchanged.

However—and we must also take this into account—by entering the market earlier, we are also taking an additional risk that we would not have taken on the basis of our original planning. In fact, we are in the market before the actual entry signal is reached. If the market falls back now, we will have to close our partial position as a losing trade. Because we are earlier in the market, we may be able to make trades that we would not have made with our original strategy.

As you already know, this naturally has an impact on our hit rate. It will inevitably deteriorate. Because if our strategy works out, we will open the second sub-position as planned. So, it makes no difference. Either way, we're in the market. However, if the strategy does not work out, we add a loser to our statistics that we would not have otherwise.

This approach will also increase the overall risk. In the event of a loss, only half of our planned risk is incurred, but due to the lower hit rate, losses will occur more often than without denomination.

The good news is that in this way we are increasing our realized risk/reward ratio. Because if our trading idea works out and we reach our profit target, then we increase our absolute profit, as we have already seen.

The trading frequency will also increase, as we will enter the market faster with a partial position than with the overall position. This means that we are not only faster, but also more often in the market.

As a result, we can state with regard to this variant that by using two sub-positions you can increase your realized risk/reward ratio, in some cases significantly. The lower hit rate and increased trading frequency are mitigated by the fact that in the event of a loss, often only half the risk is realized as a loss. What you also need to consider here are the transaction costs incurred per subitem. Depending on the product you are trading, these can quickly reduce the additional profits considerably.

We also mentioned a second option that would allow us to increase our profits while maintaining the position risk. We have already found that although we increase our profits if we enter the market earlier, we have to accept that our hit rate will fall. Maybe we can do it differently.

For example, we could gradually increase our position and thus build a pyramid, so to speak. As usual, we are entering the market here with the full size of our position and we continue to increase our position at every new opportunity. Let's take a look at the chart as well.

Figure 56: S&P 500 INDEX, weekly chart (one candle = one week). The S&P 500 fell to point 1, rose from there to point 2 and then fell back to point 3. The new trend is established with the break of point 2. Entries after each correction are at points 4, 6, 8, 10, 12, 14, 16 and even 18 result in additional chances of winning. Source: www.tradingview.com

After our entry into the S&P 500 Index with a breakout from point 2 at 1,295 points, we opened our position in full as planned. The price then moves directly in our direction and we immediately get our first book profits. The price rises to point 4 at 1,425 points to correct from there. The decline brings the S&P 500 to point 5 at 1,241 points.

However, as we have carried out our technical analysis conscientiously, we are not letting it upset us. On the contrary. For us, this is a good opportunity to increase our position at a favorable price and thus increase our chances of profit in the current just-begun trend.

We want to seize this opportunity by breaking through the last high at point 4. At first glance, it is obvious that point 5 is a new stop loss for our new position. In order not to increase the overall risk of the two positions, we trail our stop loss of the first trade underneath point 5. As a result, we now have the same stop loss for both positions.

We have to keep in mind that our first trade at point 5 is still at risk with almost a third. Of course, we do not want to increase our overall risk of both positions, but rather keep it constant. This means that we must keep the position size of our second position correspondingly smaller than the first.

As a reminder, we do not want to take a higher overall risk with the sum of our positions than was planned with the original position. This is the only way to optimize our chances of winning without taking any additional risk!

Let us look at the chart again. The S&P 500 continues its move up from point 5 and with the breakthrough of point 4 we open our second position and the according stop loss as planned.

Shortly after the breakout, the price begins to come back again from point 6 at 1,477 points and falls to point 7 at 1,318 points. This is another good opportunity for us to increase our overall position in the ongoing uptrend. We choose the break through point 6 again as next entry point and take as stop loss for the new position the last low at point 7. Of course, not exactly on the point, but always a few points below. After all, we don't want to be too quickly stopped out. The stop loss on our two existing positions is also included in point 7.

Now we have already secured our first trade with 23 points in profit and the second trade with 107 points in risk. We can determine our position size of the third trade accordingly.

After the breakout from point 6, the price rises to a new high at point 8 at 1,690 points and from there falls slightly back to point 9 at 1,535 points. Once again, we want to take the opportunity to further expand our overall position. With a break through point 8 we open our next position and set the stop loss for all current trades below point 9 at 1,535 points.

In total, we have thus secured the first trade with over 240 points, the second trade with 110 points and the third trade with 58 points in profit. We have the fourth trade at risk with 155 points. So, in the event of a stop, we have to deduct those 155 points from the overall profit.

We continue to add trade by trade to our position with every correction and every following breakout of a previous high from points 10 to 18 setting and trailing the overall stop loss from every new higher low to the next. All in all, we have the opportunity to open eight positions with a cumulated and secured profit of more than 3,000 points!

But even the most beautiful trend comes to an end at some point and so the price falls immediately after our entry at point 18 below the last low at point 19. We are stopped out at 1,879—25 points under the last low—and all positions are closed.

Risk and Money Management for Day and Swing Trading

	Entry	Stop Loss	Risk (Points)	Stop Loss 1	Risk (Points)	Stop Loss 2	Risk (Points)	Stop Loss 3	Risk (Points)	Stop Loss 4	Risk (Points)	Stop Loss 5	Risk (Points)	Stop Loss 6	Risk (Points)	Stop Loss 7	Risk (Points)
Position 1	1,295	1,133	-162	1,241	-54	1,318	23	1,535	240	1,602	307	1,712	417	1,789	494	1,879	584
Position 2	1,425			1,241	-184	1,318	-107	1,535	110	1,602	177	1,712	287	1,789	364	1,879	454
Position 3	1,477					1,318	-159	1,535	58	1,602	125	1,712	235	1,789	312	1,879	402
Position 4	1,690							1,535	-155	1,602	-88	1,712	22	1,789	99	1,879	189
Position 5	1,712									1,602	-110	1,712	0	1,789	77	1,879	167
Position 6	1,852											1,712	-140	1,789	-63	1,879	27
Position 7	1,900													1,789	-111	1,879	-21
Position 8	1,994															1,879	-115
Profit																	3,566

Figure 57: An overview of the individual trades of the overall position. Entry price, stop loss and trailing stop with the corresponding risk or accumulated profit. 3 points are always added to the entry prices in order not to trade the direct high point. The stop loss always includes a safety buffer of 25 points to the corresponding low point.

As a result, we can report a total profit of 3,566 points! If we now compare this with the result that we only achieved with the first position alone, then at first glance the result is a gamechanger. With the pyramid, the trailing stop and the addition of seven more trades we have earned nearly 3,000 points more than we would have had with the first position as a single one. Please notice also that we were in a total profit from trade number four on.

One last note. The calculation was deliberately presented in points to give you a feeling for the basic procedure. In practice, of course, the corresponding position size is also part of the points, so that the real results are different.

An important point that becomes clear is that you are well advised to reduce the position size a little with each new position—simply so as not to jeopardize the accumulated profits. Imagine this method like a pyramid. The first trade forms the basis and represents the largest position. The second trade, for example, is only allocated with 75% of the actual position size. The third trade then still with 50% and the fourth trade perhaps with only 25% of the original position size. By doing so you ensure that you maximize your profit potential while protecting your accumulated profits. Always remember that even the most beautiful trend will end at some point and the danger of a correction increases over time.

In practice, you will regularly experience that the last trade is a loser. For this reason, the pyramid is pointed at the top and the positions taken are correspondingly smaller.

In trading practice, you will regularly come up against the limits of the feasibility of this strategy due to the limited divisibility of lots, shares, ETFs or futures. An infinite pyramid structure cannot be realized in practice. A two- or three-level pyramid, on the other hand, often does. This should also be enough to accompany a trend long enough before it finally turns.

As a rule of thumb, we can state that the larger your account and thus the risk you take, the larger the positions to be split will be—and the easier it will be for you to build a pyramid.

What does the pyramid structure mean for our "Money Management Matrix"? If we are very precise, then we have to count every single position for itself. Accordingly, we are increasing our trading frequency with the pyramidization. As we take a trend to the last with more and more new positions, we will also be able to slightly increase our hit rate. The fact that the last trade regularly loses does not change that much. On the other hand, our realized risk/reward ratio will decline overall because we will always have a big winner with us, but also many smaller ones, as we have seen above.

This means: high trading frequency, high hit rate and lower risk/reward ratio. In sum, a pyramid is therefore a good way to improve trading results as long as we keep the realized risk/reward ratio above 1.

What remains is to consider the risk. If we build the pyramid correctly, the overall risk will never be higher than the individual risk. On the contrary: with each new step of the pyramid, the risk is reduced as the positions become smaller. At the same time, the stops of the positions already running are trailed to the new stop loss. The bottom line is that while we take more positions, we do not increase our overall risk. From this aspect, too, there is nothing to be said against a professionally constructed pyramid.

As a conclusion, we can state that by gradually increasing the positions, we can exploit our profit potential of a movement to the maximum. The entry with a partial position gives you best chances with unchanged risk. The prerequisite, however, is a corresponding position size that is divisible. But here, many traders already reach their limits. Therefore, always choose a product or underlying for your trading that allows you to split your position.

When building a pyramid, this challenge is intensified. This is because with each step, smaller amounts must be put at risk, which requires smaller position sizes. With pyramidization, sophisticated risk management is crucial for success. Particularly under the aspect that the susceptibility to corrections increases with the course of time and thus the danger of being stopped out increases, position sizing is the be-all and end-all. In case of doubt, it is better to remain defensive in this respect!

In connection with step-by-step trading, we have only dealt with the entry point—the scaling in. In the next step, let us also look at the exit—the scaling out. Even with a gradual exit from a position, we can improve our overall result.

Let us look directly at a chart again:

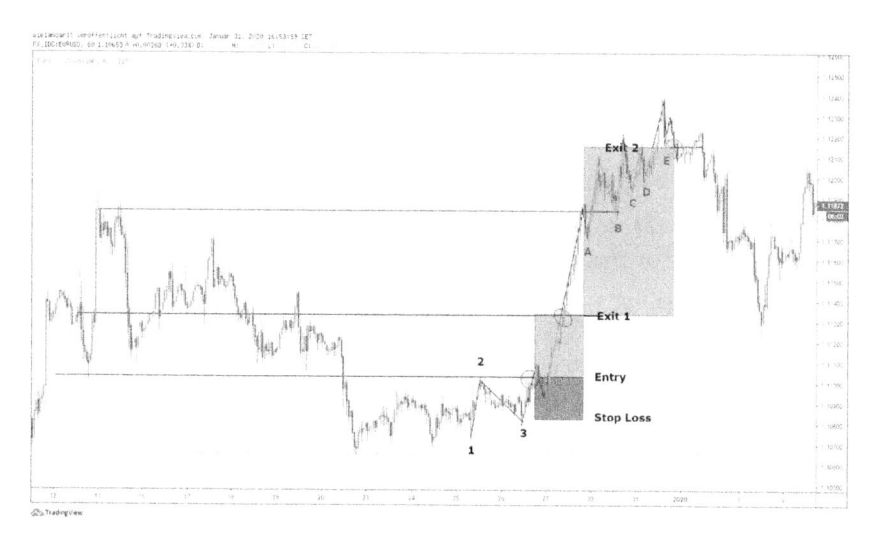

Figure 58: EUR/USD, 60-minutes chart (one candle = 60 Minutes). The price of the currency broke out of a range and went over into a steep rally, reaching the first target in one bold move. Then it went higher up to the major resistance. After breaking through, the way up was interrupted by several short corrections. The lows of the corrections provide good reference points for a trailing stop. The squares show the risk/reward ratio and the additional profit achieved with the sub-position. Source: www.tradingview.com

We are trading EUR/USD, and are speculating on a rising Euro. After bottoming out at point 1, the pair initially rose to point 2 and then dropped back to point 3. From there the currency pair sets off again it way up north.

We want to choose the breach through point 2 at $1.11023 as our entry signal and open our position when this point is crossed. The stop loss is set under point 3, and we have set ourselves the profit target with a planned risk/reward ratio of 1.5. This means that with a risk of 21 pips we want to make a profit of rounded 32 pips. So, we place the profit target at $1.11343.

A glance at the chart tells us that there are several hurdles to overcome on the way to the target, which we can identify as a major resistance slightly above point 2 followed by a resistance built by some former lows. Because the pair can experience some corrections here the profit target of a 1.5 RRR corresponds pretty good to our technical analysis. You already know this classic scenario from previous trades.

So far, we have always achieved good results, because a good planned and realized risk/reward ratio already takes us a long way forward in our success planning.

We now want to choose a different exit strategy. For this purpose, we set our profit target as described. But there we only want to exit just with half of our position. We also want to leave the other half well-secured.

Let's get back to our trade. The price rises quickly and without hesitation after our entry. As the pair rockets higher, our profit target is reached. As planned, we are exiting half of our position and realizing the profit. We have thus achieved a realized risk/reward ratio of 1.5 for this part of the position. We'll let the rest of the position go. Now we can trail the stop loss until the partial position is stopped out.

So, we want to trail the stop loss of the remaining sub-position below each newly created higher low. Now that we have unwound the first half of our position, the price is falling back again somewhat to the point A. This point now forms the new stop loss. When the lows B, C and D are marked after a further rise, we move our stop loss below these points as well.

With a stop loss under point E at $1.12160, we are already 123 pips in profit if we close the position at this point.

From Point E the EUR/USD continues to rise, but doesn't reach new a new high. Instead it fell below the last low into our trailing stop loss at $1.12160. At this point we realize a profit with our remaining sub-position of 123 pips. Together with the first half of our position, this brings us to a realized risk/reward ratio of 3.7! If we now compare this result with what we would have achieved without splitting the position, the advantage of this strategy becomes clear.

To complete the consideration, we can also look at a calculation for this trade. As mentioned at the beginning, such a strategy can only be depicted from a certain size of your trading account. For the sake of simplicity, we therefore take an account with $20,000 trading capital as the basis for our calculations. We want to take 1% of this as risk, which gives an absolute risk amount of $200—or to make it practical for our calculation $210. In forex we can trade one lot or $100,000[15] under this risk profile. This amount at risk forms the basis of the following calculation.

	Single Position	Position Part 1	Position Part 2	Total Profit
Entry	$1.11023			
Stop Loss	$1.10810		$1.12260	
Risk in Pips	21			
Profit Target	$1.11343	$1.11343		
Profit in Pips	32			
RRR planned	1.5			
Profit Pips 1.Part		32		
Profit Pips 2.Part			123	
RRR Realized	1.5	1.5	5.9	3.7

Position size	$100,000	$50,000	$50,000	
Risk absolute	$210			
Profit absolute	$320			
Profit 1. Part		$160		
Profit 2. Part			$615	$775

Figure 59: The calculation of our trade in EUR/USD. Based on a trading account with $20,000 and a risk to be taken in the amount of 1%, the results are displayed

---

[15] One Lot equals $100,000 in EUR/USD. One Mini Lot is then $10,000 and one Micro Lot is $1,000.

with a single position and with splitting the position. Due to the split position, the total profit could be increased significantly.

We see in the calculation that we have realized a risk/reward ratio of 5.9 with the second sub-position. That's more than respectable. Despite the undoubtedly good results, however, we must again point out that, as is unfortunately the case, we do not always realize profits with our remaining sub-position, but will also regularly experience that the price triggers the stop loss at an early stage. Such really good results are therefore not self-evident.

You should realize that by splitting the position, you are preserving the chance of additional profits, but if these do not occur, then you will have done significantly worse in total than if you liquidate the position as a whole.

This leads us directly to a critical examination using the "Money Management Matrix." Due to the scaling out in case of a win, our hit rate remains unchanged. The trade is a hit, whether halved or whole. However, this presupposes that we regard the two sub-positions as one trade. Since we opened the trade as a single entity, we can also proceed in this way. The hit rate therefore remains unchanged. What is the trading frequency? It also remains unchanged. The distribution in the event of a win does not change this. But what changes are the transaction costs. They are increased by the costs of closing the remaining position. Costs fundamentally increase the risk, because that is what they are. Apart from this, the position risk remains unaffected. If the stop loss is moved to the entry point as soon as the profit target is reached, the risk is eliminated. The only risk that remains is that the remaining sub-position will not make a profit, but will be stopped at the entry point with break-even—which, of course, has direct consequences on the realized risk/reward ratio. This is because if the remaining sub-position does not make a profit, but closes around break even, then the realized risk/reward ratio is halved! Compared to the original risk, we only achieve half of what we need to trade profitably!

Let's let this insight have some effect. Assuming we maximize our profits, we take the risk of halving our realized risk/reward ratio. This results in an essential consequence for you. Only use this method if you are trading a market or value that is in a strong trend phase. The further the trend goes, the more closely you have to look for reversal signals. These can be candle patterns or formations. This strategy also requires professional trade management!

In connection with a scaling-out, let's look at another idea that we can use to professionally manage our results. This strategy is not so much about maximizing profits—we will not achieve that with this strategy—but rather about minimizing losses. Accordingly, we then look at how we can unwind partial positions when we are not in profit but in a loss.

Let's take a look at another chart:

Figure 60: ALIBABA GROUP HOLDINGS LTD. (BABA), weekly chart (one candle = one week). BABA showed first reversal tendencies by marking a new interim high and correcting to a higher low. The breakout from point 2 should continue the trend. A scaling-out in loss reduces the total loss. Source: www.tradingview.com

Let us assume that we want to trade BABA. In order to obtain a calm and solid basis for decision-making, we choose the weekly chart as the setting for our chart analysis. We can see that BABA has corrected within an uptrend to point 1 at $164.25. From there the share climbed back to a newer high at $206.20 and got sold again to a higher low at point 3 at $166.13. We want to speculate on a further rise and open the trade when point 2 is exceeded. To our detriment, BABA is not performing as we would like, but is doing exactly the opposite. It begins to fall immediately after initial hesitation. Everything looks as if we are running into our stop loss, which we have placed below point 1 at $164.20. Usually it would be underneath point 3, but as 1 and 3 are very close, we decided to make it a little bit more safe and give the market a little bit more space for its movements.

Basically, this is not a big issue, because our professional risk management protects us from unplanned losses. But that does not mean that we enjoy losing and that we simply have to stand by and watch the trade become a loser. But we don't want to get out of it so directly either, because we have already talked about the fact that it is rather counterproductive to disrupt a trade. Maybe the market just needs some air to breathe.

So, what can we do apart from waiting to see how the trade is stopped out? We can also operate an active trade management in the event of losses. In the event of a loss, it may also be advisable to divide your position into sub-positions. A good possibility to implement this professionally is, for example, the partial exit according to technical chart criteria.

On the chart, the price at point A forms at least a first up move as it forms a green candle and a reversal from point A to C here. We can take this green candle and reversal as an opportunity to reduce our position. To do this, we set the stop loss for our partial position—for example, half of the total position—under point C at 184.75. If the price falls below point C, we will exit with half of our position. We then take the first loss and leave the other half unchanged. This remaining half is still protected by the original stop loss.

Our advantage within this strategy is that we can reduce our loss while at the same time preserve the chance for a positive result. In this way, we do justice to both our risk and our money management.

However, we have to make sure here that we do not make the partial exit too early. A position reduced in this way has little chance of passing the finish line as a big winner. This is because, even if the result is still positive, we first have to deduct the loss of the dissolved sub-position from the profit of the remaining sub-position. In the best case, a profit remains, but as a rule of thumb we can be happy if we end up just breaking even and do not have to bear our transaction costs ourselves. For this reason, we must not act hastily, but always consciously and according to fixed criteria. At this point, the charting technique serves us well to determine at which point the probability is more strongly against us.

Let us also look at the result in terms of concrete figures:

	Single Position	Position Part 1	Position Part 2	Total Profit
Entry	$206.20			
Stop Loss	$164.20	$184.75	$164.20	
Risk in USD	$42.00	$21.45	$42.00	

Number of Shares	11	6	5	
Positionsize	$2,268.20			
Risk absolute	$462.00			
Loss absolute	-$462.00	-$128.70	-$210.00	-$338.70

Figure 61: By dissolving a partial position, the overall loss is reduced by more than 26%.

The figures speak for themselves. Assuming we take a $50,000 trading account as a basis and risk 1% of our trading account for this trade as usual, we can buy 11 shares of BABA. By selling one half—6 of 11 shares—we were able to reduce our loss by 26.7%. After all. A loss saved is almost like a gain. It increases the financial basis for our next trade!

The Time-Warp: How to link different time frames

Although we are now very advanced in our considerations and are at a very high professional level, you can add another idea to your existing knowledge.

Up to now, we have always assumed that we are moving within a single time frame. The entrances and exits were all in one single time frame. For example, the analysis of an underlying was only done in the 60-minutes, 4-hour, daily, or weekly chart. Accordingly, the entry and exit points were determined in the same chart as well. This is only plausible and has proven to bring us clearly positive results.

And this is precisely the point at which we want to start with our further considerations. We have already noticed with the trading styles that they are used in different time frames. But why should we only commit ourselves to one time frame, when we can also look beyond the horizon? Maybe we can improve our results here without having to change our chosen trading style.

What possibilities arise for you if you look at two or three time frames instead of just one? The consideration of different time frames has several advantages for you.

On one hand, this allows you to identify hidden resistances and supports that lie in other time frames. You can improve your hit rate by choosing your trades even more consciously and selectively. On the other hand, you can refine your entries by searching for entry signals not only in your preferred time frame, but also in those below it. This gives you the opportunity to score a few more points and find cleaner entrances. You can also define your stop loss more narrowly, for example, by searching for concrete levels for your stop loss in a subordinate time frame. The second point in particular can help you to move forward with your money management without having to change your risk significantly.

Let's have a look at the first variant right away. Imagine you are conducting a thorough analysis of an underlying in your preferred time frame. You identify a good entry opportunity according to your trading strategy and set an entry, just as you set your stop loss and profit target. When your entry is triggered, you open the trade. The market maintains the preferred direction, the position runs into a profit, and everything looks like a successful trade by now. But suddenly the momentum slows down, the market initially moves sideways, and then corrects sharply. Your initial winner is now in danger of becoming a loser.

What happened? Perhaps you missed some important news? Or did you not conduct your analysis correctly after all? What else should you have considered?

We experience this described situation regularly and the reasons for this are many. We have already discussed the fact that something like this can happen on several occasions, and that is precisely why we have established our risk management system. Nevertheless, we can at least partly avoid these situations. If we no longer limit our analysis to a single time frame, but also include the neighboring ones, we can certainly avoid a potential loser once in a while.

Let's take a look at the INTEL CORP on the 15-minute chart for a clearer picture.

Risk and Money Management for Day and Swing Trading

Figure 62: INTEL CORP, 15-minute chart (one candle = 15 minutes). Intel has been in a good uptrend for a while and suddenly breaks out of its channel just to go even higher. What a bullish move! After making a new high the price fell and moved slowly but steadily down towards marking a lower low. Source: www.tradingview.com

In Intel, we see the situation just as described. With the open of the market the price opens with a solid price gap and remains positive within the first fifteen minutes. A possible strategy for day trader is an entry after the first fifteen minutes with a break of the high or low of that period. As the price continuous to rise we open our position at $58.76 including a 5-cent security buffer. We place our stop loss underneath the low of the 15-minute period at $58.08 including the same buffer. If the price falls below the low point, a positive outcome of our trading idea would be neglected and the probability that the uptrend will continue would no longer exist. With entering the market, the trade runs directly into a good profit and the stock rises up to a new high. Fine – but suddenly the upward momentum comes to an abrupt end and the price begins to fall dynamically. The incipient downward movement leads our trade after several hours and days into the stop loss and the position is closed marking a loser. As things develop, the price moves sideways for a while before falling further closing the gap. An up move is no longer relevant, at least not in the short term.

The question that arises at this point is if we could have avoided this scenario. The answer is mixed: Yes and no. Because on the 15-minute chart there was no further indication that the up move might encounter an obstacle. And this is where the other time frames come into play. For what could be more obvious, we could shift the analysis from the 15-minute chart to the daily chart. Maybe we could have found a clue there.

Let's take a look at the daily chart right away:

Figure 63: INTEL CORP, daily chart (one candle = one day). After a downtrend, Intel has gone volatile sideways for an extended period of time before breaking upward. Source: www.tradingview.com

That's not what it looks like. We can see that after a strong bullish move Intel reaches the area where it has been before and where all the trouble started. This is a major resistance! The day before the price gap—which is the day before we opened our trade—the price forms a certain candlestick in a remarkable area. The candlestick is known as Doji and it indicates at least uncertainty in the market. In a very sensitive area like the major resistance it says something like "Wait, we are not so sure about the next move." So, this is the area we are trying to open a trade speculating on higher prices.

So, we bought right into a resistance! And to make it worse, we bought near the absolute high of the day. This resistance was not visible on the 15-minute chart as it was too far from the entry point in relation to the time frame. On the daily chart, however, it is. Based on this information, would you have opened the trade with speculation on rising prices? Probably not. Maybe you would have chosen the other direction instead.

The comparison of 15-minute charts with daily charts alone has already brought us clarity. For the sake of completeness, let us take a look at the next time frame above, the weekly chart:

Figure 64: INTEL CORP, weekly chart (one candle = one week). Intel is in a long-term uptrend interrupted by a correction which was ended and now comes to a strong barrier. Source: www.tradingview.com

We can see that Intel is in a long term steep bullish move, which came to an abrupt end. After a sharp correction, the subsequent sideways movement can also be seen on the weekly chart. In addition, it can be seen that the price rises with high momentum into the area of the former high. In hindsight we now see that it would be a far better idea to choose the opposite direction and go short instead of buying. But we also see that trading without a stop loss is more than dangerous and includes the danger of wiping out your trading account at once.

We can draw several conclusions from this triple screen analysis:

First of all, it is important to identify hidden resistance or support levels to avoid a trade being doomed to failure from the outset. For you, this means that you should always turn up at least one time frame to make sure that there are no hidden obstacles to your trading idea.

Second, we can determine the basic trend direction by analyzing over several time frames. You can then better determine in your analysis whether you are trading with the superior trend or whether your trade is just a correction of the superior trend. Depending on this, you will of course have to determine and set your profit target.

Third, this form of analysis helps us to look beyond the horizon. You can use this again in several ways.

A good opportunity is a good opportunity! So, if you see that there is a good trade waiting for you in a lower time frame, there is no reason why you should not check it according to your criteria and implement it. Additionally, this method helps you to improve the timing of your trades. As we have seen above, the idea of entering into an up move was not fundamentally wrong. But the management was. Obviously, it would have been better to set a moderate profit target rather than hoping for the next big move. On the other hand, if you get into the trade and take the loss and then realize the opportunities lie now on the other side, why not go that way? This brings us to a very important insight. Always remember: Up or down—it is the market which tells you which way to go!

Perhaps you are now wondering what this consideration has to do with risk and money management. Of course, a lot. We have already seen how important it is for you to pay attention to the quality of your trades. Your goal must be to keep the elements of the "Money Management Matrix" at a constantly high level. This also includes keeping an eye on the hit rate. If you now exclude at least a few of the trades that are doomed to failure through this type of analysis, then this has an immediate positive effect on your hit rate. It's going to go up—especially if you can identify some profitable opportunities that you might not have found otherwise.

For this reason alone, it is worthwhile to compare several time frames with each other and thus get a better overview of what is happening in the market. And we can also take a look at another positive effect of this idea.

The second positive effect you get by analyzing different time frames is the refinement of your entries and/or exits. This allows you to search for an entry at a lower time frame after or even before your actual signal is triggered, thus optimizing the potential for profit. Or you can still find an entry into a trade even if you have missed the actual entry signal. To do this, use the correction in a lower time frame following the breakout. From there you can still enter the market, even if there is no possibility to open a position in your preferred time frame.

Let's take a look at a concrete situation in this regard. We want to trade the S&P 500 Index for the longer term and therefore conduct our analysis in the weekly chart.

Figure 65: S&P 500 INDEX, weekly chart (one candle = one week). Starting from a sharp decline at point 1, the S&P 500 rises up as fast as it fell down. In the area of the former high the price pulls back and corrects to the point 3. From there the uptrend continuous. Source: www.tradingview.com

After falling back to 2,346.58 points at point 1, the S&P 500 rises continuously to point 2 at 2,954.13 points marking a slightly higher high. The price then bounces off the resistance and falls back to the point 3 at 2,728.81 points. The last high at point 2 marks in combination with the other former high a strong resistance. With the big green candlestick embracing the red one we can be positive that the move up will continue. So, we want to use this opportunity to enter the market and open a trade. We want to use the breakout from the last high at point 2 at 2,945.13 points to open a position. Our stop loss will be under point 3 at 2,728.81 points. So much for the classic approach that we have used throughout up to now.

We now want to go down into a lower time frame to see if we can get into the market a little bit earlier. Maybe we can shorten the distance between the entry point and the stop loss a bit.

Figure 66: S&P 500 INDEX, daily chart (one candle = one day). The S&P 500 is in an uptrend that is repeatedly interrupted by pullbacks and lateral movements. Source: www.tradingview.com

The S&P 500 in the daily chart gives us a more detailed picture and we see what happened in detail in each individual week. Since we have already completed the long-term analysis in the weekly chart, we can concentrate on the immediate time before our entry point for the detailed work.

We can see that the S&P 500 has fallen from point 1 at 2,954.13 points to point 4 at 2,728.81 points. We have already noted this in the weekly chart. There, point 1 corresponds to our point 4 or A in the daily chart. In contrast to the weekly chart, where it appears that the S&P 500 has fallen steeply without interruption and only stopped at the low of 2,728.81 points, we see in the daily chart that the decline was accompanied by a short correction from point 2 to 3.

To find our entry point in the daily chart, we can again look for a point where the probability of a further rise is greater than the probability of a further fall in the price. This is in the area of point 3 at 2,892.15 to B at 2,910.61 points. If the price rises above it, the sequence of lower highs and lows has been broken and there is a chance for a continuation of the uptrend.

By doing so we can set our entry point above point B at 2,910.61 points. This also provides us with a safety buffer in case the market makes an attempt at deception. We can leave the stop loss at 2,728.81 points—as planned in the weekly chart—or better still slightly below it at 2,725 points or even 2,720 points.

If we compare, then by changing the time frames we can move the entry from 2,954.13 points to 2,910.61 points. This gives us an advantage of 43.52 points!

Finally, our analysis of the two time frames allows us to complete our overall picture by superimposing both analysis.

Figure 67: S&P 500 INDEX, weekly chart (one candle = one week). The results of the daily and the weekly chart are shown. This further refines the greater picture. Source: www.tradingview.com

If we combine the findings from the weekly and daily chart analysis, we can also assess exactly how the entry into the position in the daily chart should be done. Perhaps you have already noticed that we have practically bought into an upcoming resistance. In the daily chart this has a greater relevance than in the weekly chart. The weekly chart shows the superior uptrend and this supports our view that the up move should continue. Accordingly, we can also classify the chance that the resistance will be broken as high. The trade is justified.

Let us take a closer look to the different management possibilities both time frames offer. Using the weekly chart, the stop loss is determined to be under point 3, the low of the price correction from where the uptrend continues. Looking at the weekly chart, there is no other reasonable option. But if you go deeper into the daily chart, you will find several options for a stop loss. One option is a really tight one under point C at 2,874.68 points. Of course, this one is pretty aggressive and the risk of being stopped out is much higher than in the weekly chart. But we also have to consider that the position size with such a tight stop loss is much bigger than the size with a wider stop loss. So, again the question is what you want to achieve in trading and if you are rather aggressive or defensive as a trader. Also keep in mind that if you decide to use a tight stop loss, you can on the one hand use a higher position size but you are also likely to being stopped out much earlier compared to the wider stop loss.

Looking at the daily chart you will see that with a tighter stop, you will either exit the trade with a small profit or with your planned loss—depending on your trade management. If you use the wider stop loss instead, you will be able to capture the long and more lucrative move of a market. But you will also have to go through several price corrections during your trade. So, again, professional and successful trading is a matter of individual preferences.

Here, too, you may be wondering about the relevance to our topic, risk and money management. This is, of course, given. The influence on the elements of the "Money Management Matrix" can be felt immediately.

By refining your entries, you can definitely increase your realized risk/reward ratio, because you simply get more for the same risk if you win. The hit rate could drop slightly, as you always run the risk of getting a false signal if you start earlier. We have already discussed this above. This disadvantage is outweighed by the higher risk/reward ratio, so that this two-stage procedure is definitely sensible from a money management perspective. The trading frequency could also increase somewhat, as there is, of course, the danger of simply entering positions too early, which then do not trigger the actual trading signal, but instead run into a loss. In this case you open a position that you would not have opened in your actual time frame. In this sense, the overall risk must then be taken into account, even if the risk per position does not increase.

Taken together, a significantly higher realized risk/reward ratio is offset by a possibly decreased hit rate and a conceivably increased trading frequency with a higher overall risk. We have already emphasized on several occasions that the realized risk/reward ratio is the measure of all things for us. Accordingly, this potential advantage outweighs the possible disadvantages. Of course, you must always check your results in this regard and take immediate countermeasures if your overall results deteriorate.

A brief summary of the most important facts:

> The use of a trailing stop can, if used correctly, secure your accrued profits.
> A step-by-step entry into a position can secure you further profits without increasing your risk.
> Increasing your position gradually in the form of a pyramid allows you to maximize your profits in an existing trend.
> A trend is absolutely necessary if you decide at the profit target to let a partial position run further. A trailing stop secures the accumulated profits of the remaining sub-position.
> In the event of a loss, you reduce your overall loss by liquidating a partial position, which preserves your valuable capital for the next trade.
> Analysis over several time frames opens up the whole picture and helps you to identify hidden resistance or support.
> By using subordinate time frames, you can refine your entries and thus achieve a higher risk/reward ratio.

CHAPTER 7:
Success Can Be Planned In Small Steps to the Big Goal!

We have come a long way in our discussions and you have dealt extensively with the elements of professional risk and money management. Not only that, but you have also learned concrete techniques that allow you to professionally manage your trades in consideration of the "Money Management Matrix." This gives you the tools you need to achieve sustained success on the financial markets.

And this leads us to the next point. Many investors and traders associate trading with the dream of big money, financial freedom, and the profession of a professional trader!

The good news is that this is possible. The bad is that it needs many conditions to actually achieve this. In addition to professional risk and money management, this naturally includes a profitable strategy with a positive expected value. In order to develop this strategy, you need a sound knowledge of the methods of fundamental and chart technical analysis. The big picture only opens up to you when you link all the components in your analysis. This is especially true if you choose a longer-term trading style. For this reason, further literature on this subject is highly recommended.

In addition to knowledge of the hard facts, this also includes knowledge of the person carrying out the work. That's you! We have looked at your personal requirements to make sure that your trading style, trading strategy, and risk management really suit you and you feel comfortable in your "trader skin." Only then can your trading be truly successful. I recommend that you consult further literature on this subject as well.

Besides all the knowledge about trading, the markets, and yourself, I would like to take a closer look at two points: your trading discipline and your trading capital.

We have already discussed your trading capital in detail and the aim of professional risk and money management is not only to protect it, but also to increase it. We will deal with this point in more detail later in this chapter.

Trading discipline is another matter. That too has been heard over and over again. Discipline comes from within and can only be maintained permanently if you approach your trading with motivation and concentration—every day anew. This is precisely why it is important for you to deal conscientiously with risk and money management. Professional management provides you with the mental basis to pursue your trading in a motivated and disciplined manner day after day.

How can that be? To what extent does risk and money management support you in maintaining your motivation and discipline for trading? By preventing disproportionate losses through risk management. By remaining mentally capable of acting, even if you have had to accept a series of losses. In this sense, strict risk management helps you to remain calm and act objectively when the market runs against you. Strictly speaking, your most human emotions in trading are hindering or even being harmful to your trading success, because neither fear nor greed should determine your trading decisions.

Professional risk and money management protects you from these emotions. If executed correctly, you know everything before you open your position. You know how much you can lose. You also know how much you can win. You´re sure of it—no matter what direction the market takes after your trade opens. You already know what the outcome will be for you under normal circumstances—in both the positive and negative sense. This is the security you need to be able to make rational decisions. The only thing you can do after you have opened your position is to professionally manage your trade.

Throughout the book we have talked about losing again and again, and with good reason. After all, loss is as much a part of trading as costs are of sales. Of course, everyone wants to keep their costs as low as possible in order to increase their profits. However, it is generally not possible to avoid costs. Costs or losses are an integral part of a trading strategy. This is also an important point that needs to be internalized.

Perhaps the following approach will also help you to deal with losses:

We have dealt with the expected value in the previous chapter. A positive expectation value means that on average each individual trade generates a certain profit. This means that you can expect a profit with every trade—whether closed in profit or loss—within a strategy. Or in other words: Every trade brings you one step closer to your profit! You can also use this attitude in many other areas of your life!

In general, we can say that every failure you overcome brings you one step closer to the desired success.

Once again—a single trade is not decisive; it always depends on the total amount!

And we want to continuously increase the total amount through money management. We have also discussed this sufficiently and you already know a number of elements with which you can work here. Let's dig a little deeper at this point.

How can you increase your capital base? How can you take advantage of the discussed mechanisms to grow your trading account?

In the course of calculating the size of the position, we have determined that the percentage approach to the trading account is the most appropriate for our purposes. By fixing the percentage amount in relation to your trading account, you keep the absolute amount variable. For example, you always risk 1% of your trading account. In this context, we have also made it clear that this approach acts like a brake and accelerator on your trading account. If your account increases because you are in a period of repeated wins, then your absolute risk taken increases with each new trade. This is simply because your trading account will grow in size, increasing the base to which the 1% rule applies. You practically turn on the turbo!

The same effect also works the other way around, of course. As soon as a phase with losses occurs, the percentage fix slows down the financial decline with each new trade. The absolute amount at risk decreases from position to position until a trend reversal occurs and you realize profits again.

This consideration alone is worth underlining in green. However, it becomes really interesting if you are aware of the laws of mathematics in this context. Because you can use this effect of brake and accelerator to consistently build and expand your trading account!

In order to really be able to exercise the profession of a professional trader, you need a certain financial basis. Based on the example accounts of Anna, Rick, and Peter, you have certainly already noticed that none of the three accounts is suitable for ensuring a permanent income through trading on its own.

In this context, we can take a look at how much income is possible in the various account sizes, and which account size can lead to which results.

Return per time unit	10%	20%	30%	40%	50%
Account size	Return	Return	Return	Return	Return
$5,000	$500	$1,000	$1,500	$2,000	$2,500
$15,000	$1,500	$3,000	$4,500	$6,000	$7,500
$25,000	$2,500	$5,000	$7,500	$10,000	$12,500
$50,000	$5,000	$10,000	$15,000	$20,000	$25,000
$100,000	$10,000	$20,000	$30,000	$40,000	$50,000

Figure 68: The table of returns.

Risk and Money Management for Day and Swing Trading

As you can see, the above five account sizes already need to be traded very professionally and with lasting positive results to ensure a life as a professional trader. Of course, you know best how much return you can earn per time unit. And it makes a difference, of course, whether you get 10% return per day, week, month or year. Even if you achieve 10% return—i.e., profit—per year through your trading, that is more than respectable. However, you will not achieve financial freedom from a standing position with the account sizes listed above.

The whole thing becomes even worse when the tax to be deducted is taken into account. Then the result is reduced accordingly. In order to keep the observation simple and true for anyone, we will refrain from this representation. However, you can easily calculate the tax effects on your trading results in your own calculations.

Maybe now you'll say, "Ten percent? I do it every week." Then please also note that the markets have phases in which there is high volatility and then again have phases in which there is low volatility. What do you want to live on during these weak phases? Do not put yourself under pressure and do not trade under duress! This will have a direct impact on your results—a negative one. This in turn reduces your financial base and puts you under even more pressure.

Perhaps the above account sizes may not be directly suited to lead a comfortable life as a trader. However, they are all a good point to start growing such an account size.

In this context, simply imagine that you generate a return of 10% in the long term—year after year. You continue to pursue your profession and leave the profits earned on your trading account. How do you think your account will develop?

Let's take a look at how your account will develop if you start with—say—$10,000 trading capital. What results can be achieved?

Time unit	Starting capital	Return	Final capital time unit
1	$10,000.00	$1,000.00	$11,000.00
2	$11,000.00	$1,100.00	$12,100.00
3	$12,100.00	$1,210.00	$13,310.00
4	$13,310.00	$1,331.00	$14,641.00
5	$14,641.00	$1,464.10	$16,105.10
6	$16,105.10	$1,610.51	$17,715.61
7	$17,715.61	$1,771.56	$19,487.17
8	$19,487.17	$1,948.72	$21,435.89
9	$21,435.89	$2,143.59	$23,579.48
10	$23,579.48	$2,357.95	$25,937.42
11	$25,937.42	$2,593.74	$28,531.17
12	$28,531.17	$2,853.12	$31,384.28
13	$31,384.28	$3,138.43	$34,522.71
14	$34,522.71	$3,452.27	$37,974.98
15	$37,974.98	$3,797.50	$41,772.48
16	$41,772.48	$4,177.25	$45,949.73
17	$45,949.73	$4,594.97	$50,544.70
18	$50,544.70	$5,054.47	$55,599.17
19	$55,599.17	$5,559.92	$61,159.09
20	$61,159.09	$6,115.91	$67,275.00
21	$67,275.00	$6,727.50	$74,002.50
22	$74,002.50	$7,400.25	$81,402.75
23	$81,402.75	$8,140.27	$89,543.02
24	$89,543.02	$8,954.30	$98,497.33
25	$98,497.33	$9,849.73	$108,347.06
26	$108,347.06	$10,834.71	$119,181.77
27	$119,181.77	$11,918.18	$131,099.94
28	$131,099.94	$13,109.99	$144,209.94
29	$144,209.94	$14,420.99	$158,630.93
30	$158,630.93	$15,863.09	$174,494.02

Risk and Money Management for Day and Swing Trading

Figure 69: A trading account that starts with $10,000 and generates 10% return year after year can grow to more than $174,000 before taxes after 30 years.

If you earn 10% every year through your trading, you can build your account up to more than $174,000 in 30 years. That actually looks pretty good. And with this result you will already beat the usual capital investments by far. But maybe you will reach the 10% per quarter? Or actually a month?

What does the result look like if you generate a return of 25% year after year?

Time unit	Starting capital	Return	Final capital time unit
1	$10,000.00	$2,500.00	$12,500.00
2	$12,500.00	$3,125.00	$15,625.00
3	$15,625.00	$3,906.25	$19,531.25
4	$19,531.25	$4,882.81	$24,414.06
5	$24,414.06	$6,103.52	$30,517.58
6	$30,517.58	$7,629.39	$38,146.97
7	$38,146.97	$9,536.74	$47,683.72
8	$47,683.72	$11,920.93	$59,604.64
9	$59,604.64	$14,901.16	$74,505.81
10	$74,505.81	$18,626.45	$93,132.26
11	$93,132.26	$23,283.06	$116,415.32
12	$116,415.32	$29,103.83	$145,519.15
13	$145,519.15	$36,379.79	$181,898.94
14	$181,898.94	$45,474.74	$227,373.68
15	$227,373.68	$56,843.42	$284,217.09
16	$284,217.09	$71,054.27	$355,271.37
17	$355,271.37	$88,817.84	$444,089.21
18	$444,089.21	$111,022.30	$555,111.51
19	$555,111.51	$138,777.88	$693,889.39
20	$693,889.39	$173,472.35	$867,361.74
21	$867,361.74	$216,840.43	$1,084,202.17
22	$1,084,202.17	$271,050.54	$1,355,252.72
23	$1,355,252.72	$338,813.18	$1,694,065.89
24	$1,694,065.89	$423,516.47	$2,117,582.37
25	$2,117,582.37	$529,395.59	$2,646,977.96
26	$2,646,977.96	$661,744.49	$3,308,722.45
27	$3,308,722.45	$827,180.61	$4,135,903.06
28	$4,135,903.06	$1,033,975.77	$5,169,878.83
29	$5,169,878.83	$1,292,469.71	$6,462,348.54
30	$6,462,348.54	$1,615,587.13	$8,077,935.67

Risk and Money Management for Day and Swing Trading

Figure 70: A trading account that starts with $10,000 and generates a 25% return year after year can grow to more than $8 million before taxes after 30 years.

What does that mean to you? Of course, this result is not self-evident. Even though we have already shown several times that a result of 25% is quite possible if you optimize the elements of the "Money Management Matrix" and pay attention to the quality of your trades. Well-considered and intelligent action are the keys to success.

The basic prerequisite is of course always an appropriate profitable strategy. We have mentioned this again and again. But in the end, the most important factor is you—you are the executing trader. It's up to you to generate that amount. This also means being able to deal with the growing absolute risk. For example: If you always take a risk of 1% of your trading account per trade, then with a $10,000 trading account this is a manageable $100. But if your account grows and you then arrive at $100,000, then we are now talking about $1,000 absolute risk. If you have reached an account size of $500,000, this is $5,000 risk per trade. In percentage terms, we still have a 1% risk here. However, the reference level has increased significantly. You must be able to handle that. Because the achievement of the values outlined above can only be guaranteed if you adhere strictly and disciplined to the plan. As soon as you deviate from your plan, you risk your overall result.

Why are we working so hard on these figures? To give you a feeling for how much can be made out of a manageable amount of money if you follow a disciplined strategy and pay attention to the quality of your trades. If you consider the mechanisms of the "Money Management Matrix" in this context and optimize the elements according to your requirements, then you are well on the way to achieving your goal. Because financial mathematics will do the rest for you:

"Compound interest is the eighth wonder of the world." – Mayer Amschel Rothschild

A brief summary of the most important facts:

> Professional risk and money management can protect you from harmful emotions in trading.
> The percentage fixing of the risk in relation to your trading account acts as a brake and accelerator. In good phases you accelerate, in difficult phases you brake automatically.
> The compound interest effect can cause even small trading accounts to grow into substantial sums. Make good use of this effect!

Closing words

Dear reader! We have come to the end of our considerations and I hope you have been able to take some suggestions from this book for your personal trading practice.

We discussed a lot of points and starting from life in general, we came to trading in the financial markets. Looking back at the markets, we found that risk management is not such a bad idea if you want to be actively involved in trading tomorrow. And that exactly is my wish for you. Put what you have read and learned into practice and work intensively with it. Protect your precious financial base and build it up continuously—piece by piece until you have reached your personal trading goal. Use and optimize the elements of the "Money Management Matrix" and constantly look for improvement of its individual components.

My purpose in this book is to show you that trading is not witchcraft. You don't have to open an excessive number of trades or implement particularly exotic strategies to achieve a respectable result. Nor do you have to take a disproportionate risk.

Always remember: If you take a position risk of 1% of your trading account and execute 100 trades with a hit rate of 50% and a realized risk/reward ratio of 1.5, then this results in a total return of 25% capital growth! And you've seen in the previous chapter where a 25% return can take you if you achieve it constantly and regularly. To achieve this goal, from now on there can only be one principle for you: Quality before quantity!

What you need is a solid trading strategy, knowledge of your own trading preferences and challenges, and discipline. I am very happy to support you to build, develop and maintain these and other points.

Feel free to approach me about this. I am always happy to receive your questions, suggestions, and feedback. You can reach me via the website of the Torero Traders School or under get-ready@torero-traders-school.com. Also, you can find me on Facebook and the other social media. So, let´s get in touch!

In this sense I always wish you good trades and much success on the way to your personal trading goal!

Yours,
Wieland Arlt

About the Author

"Wieland Arlt is one of the most successful traders in Germany, a sought-after speaker and author of specialist articles and books". – Börse Online

Wieland Arlt is a Certified Financial Technician (CFTe®), coach, and trainer. As a professional trader he has been dealing with the subject of investing and trading for many years. He is a bestselling author and has also written numerous articles about trading. He is a board member of Germany's "Union of technical analysts in Germany" and is also a sought-after speaker at money shows and conferences.

As trader, coach, and trainer, it is important to him to train every trader with trading approaches that are easy to understand and therefore also easy to implement. Especially, the consideration of the individual requirements of each trader is of great importance in his trading classes.

His declared aim is to support traders in achieving their financial goals in a self-determined manner and to trade successfully on the financial markets in the long term.

Invitation to my free webinar

To learn more about Day and Swing Trading join my free webinar.

Follow the link or scan the code to register for free!

Yours Wieland Arlt

About the Torero Traders School

The Torero Traders School pursues the goal of showing traders and investors the paths to their financial goals and to support them in achieving their goals. Thereby the Torero Traders School sees itself as partner and mentor.

For this purpose, the Torero Traders School offers interested people a comprehensive education and coaching, which is implemented in form of video courses and webinars as well as in personal trainings.

The training programs of the Torero Traders School are aimed at imparting the necessary knowledge in such a way that each participant can define his own approach to his trading. As a result, investors gain the knowledge and skills to take their financial future into their own hands and make independent investment decisions.

www.torero-traders-school.com

Disclaimer and Risk Disclosure

Trading of securities or derivatives is associated with high risk of loss that may go well beyond the amount of the original investment. This is particularly true for trading with leveraged products and on margin. Past results are no indication of future performance. In no event should the content of this correspondence be construed as an explicit or implied promise or guarantee.

The from Wieland Arlt offered ideas such as analysis, strategies, market comments, views and transactions are no advice or investment services and do not constitute an offer or invitation to buy, hold or sell securities or derivatives. They are merely teaching material and are used for teaching purposes.

If the market moves against you, you may sustain a total loss greater than the amount you deposited into your account. You are responsible for risks and financial resources you use and for the chosen trading system. You should not engage in trading unless you fully understand the nature of the transactions you are entering into and the extent of your exposure to loss. If you do not fully understand these risks you must seek independent advice from your financial advisor.

Therefore Wieland Arlt accepts no liability for presented opinions, analyzes, strategies or other information. Website visitors, readers and participants of the training courses of Wieland Arlt, who make investment decisions and / or conduct transactions upon the published content, act in full own risk.

Printed in Great Britain
by Amazon